AFRICAN AMERICAN TRAILBLAZERS

Frederick Douglass

Abolitionist and Writer

Avery Elizabeth Hurt

Cavendish Square
New York

For the awesome librarians at the Birmingham Public Library, without whom I wouldn't be able to write books. It's about time I thanked them properly.

Published in 2020 by Cavendish Square Publishing, LLC
243 5th Avenue, Suite 136, New York, NY 10016

First Edition

Library of Congress Cataloging-in-Publication Data

Names: Hurt, Avery Elizabeth, author.
Title: Frederick Douglass : abolitionist and writer / Avery Elizabeth Hurt.
Description: First edition. | New York : Cavendish Square, [2020] | Series: African American trailblazers | Includes bibliographical references and index. | Audience: Grades 9-12.
Identifiers: LCCN 2018047436 (print) | LCCN 2018048582 (ebook) | ISBN 9781502645470 (ebook) | ISBN 9781502645463 (library bound) | ISBN 9781502645456 (pbk.)
Subjects: LCSH: Douglass, Frederick, 1818-1895--Juvenile literature. | Slaves--United States--Biography--Juvenile literature. | Abolitionists--United States--Biography--Juvenile literature. | African American abolitionists--Biography--Juvenile literature. | Antislavery movements--United States--History--Juvenile literature.
Classification: LCC E449.D75 (ebook) | LCC E449.D75 H87 2020 (print) | DDC 973.8092 [B] --dc23
LC record available at https://lccn.loc.gov/2018047436

Editorial Director: David McNamara
Editor: Kristen Susienka
Copy Editor: Alex Tessman
Associate Art Director: Alan Sliwinski
Designer: Joe Parenteau
Production Coordinator: Karol Szymczuk
Photo Research: J8 Media

The photographs in this book are used by permission and through the courtesy of: Cover, pp. 40-41, 92 MPI/Getty Images; p. 4 J. R. Eyerman/The LIFE Picture Collection/Getty Images; p. 7 Randy Duchaine/Alamy Stock Photo; pp. 8, 27, 99 Everett Historical/Shutterstock.com; p. 12 Mathew Brady (1822-1896) Original photographers: McPherson and Oliver. Part of the Blakeslee Collection, apparently collected by John Taylor of Hartford, Connecticut, USA/File: Cicatrices de flagellation sur un esclave.jpg/Wikimedia Commons/Public Domain; p. 19 joiseyshowaa, Freehold, NJ, USA/File: Big Dipper & North Star above Joisey (3527512498).jpg/Wikimedia Commons/CCA-SA 2.0 Generic; p. 21 Library of Congress/Getty Images; p. 23 Byron Key/Shutterstock.com; p. 24 © North Wind Picture Archives; pp. 30-31 Library of Congress, Prints & Photographs; p. 33 Photograph first published in Rosetta Douglass Sprague, "My Mother As I Recall Her", 1900, Library of Congress/File: Anna Murray-Douglass.jpg/Wikimedia Commons/Public Domain; p. 36 Cindy Hopkins/Alamy Stock Photo; p. 46 Southworth and Hawes (American, active 1843–1863) Metropolitan Museum of Art/File: William Lloyd Garrison by Southworth and Hawes, c1850.png/Wikimedia Commons/Public Domain; pp. 50-51, 53 Hulton Archive/Getty Images; pp. 56-57 Joseph Sohm/Shutterstock.com; pp. 61, 87 Bettmann/Getty Images; p. 69 Frederick Douglass, M. R. Delany (editors) Library of Congress/File: The North Star june 2 1848.png/Wikimedia Commons/Public Domain; p. 71 Hammatt Billings, http://muarchives.missouri.edu/images/exh_libraries/LE-SpecUncleTomsCabinLarge300res.jpg/File: UncleTomsCabinCover.jpg/Wikimedia Commons/Public Domain; p. 74 Fotosearch/Getty Images; p. 77 Mathew Brady (1822-1896) ebay/File: Stephen Douglas CDV by Brady.jpg/Wikimedia Commons/Public Domain; p. 83 Carol M. Highsmith/Buyenlarge/Getty Images; pp. 88-89 Universal History Archive/UIG/Getty Images; pp. 96-97 Archive Photos/Getty Images; pp. 100-101 Walter Smalling for the Historic American Buildings Survey, Library of Congress, Prints & Photographs/File: Frederick Douglass House.jpg/Wikimedia Commons/Public Domain; p. 104 Corbis/Getty Images.

Printed in the United States of America

CONTENTS

INTRODUCTION

A Man Without a Birthday

When the man now known as Frederick Douglass was born on the Eastern Shore of Maryland, his mother named him Frederick Augustus Washington Bailey. As far as he knew, his birthday was sometime in February 1817 or 1818; he couldn't be certain. He was born a slave, and no one thought it important to record the birthdates of slaves. By many during that time, they weren't thought of as people—more like complicated animals, owned by other people and used for farm work.

Life as a Slave

Douglass's life as a slave was not too different from that of most slaves in the antebellum South. He was separated

Frederick Douglass is photographed here around 1850 by J. R. Eyerman.

from his mother when he was a baby and passed from master to master throughout his childhood and young adult years. He worked hard, was treated kindly by some masters, and cruelly by others. He had no rights and no control over his own life.

However, he did one thing not many slaves managed to do, something slaves were forbidden to do: he learned to read. Once he learned, he put that new skill to good use. He educated himself using borrowed and found books. From that point on, he never stopped reading and learning.

Runaway

Douglass spent years plotting his escape, and then when he was still a young man, he ran away to the North. When he reached freedom, he changed his name to Frederick Douglass to hide from those who would try to capture him and return him to slavery. We know about him today not just because he managed to escape from slavery—he was certainly not the only slave to do that—nor because he learned to read—some other slaves managed that as well. We remember him because of what he did once he was free.

A Lion of a Man

Frederick Douglass was handsome, articulate, and intelligent, with a striking appearance. He was a great deal taller than average for the time and powerfully built, with a wild head of hair. His penetrating gaze could be both intense and thoughtful. His looks as well as his demeanor often caused people to describe him as leonine—or lion-like. This was not the image most people had of slaves—even white abolitionists, who wanted their freedom. Douglass put a human face on an outrage that many people at the time gave little thought to.

He was a natural leader as well as a gifted speaker and writer. He used these skills to convince a reluctant nation not only that slavery was wrong and must be ended, but that African Americans were as intelligent and capable of being a part of the nation as their white brothers and sisters. Douglass was one of the greatest and most effective leaders of the abolition movement. When he escaped the bonds of slavery and settled in the North, he stepped into the greatest political debate the United States has ever had, and he shaped the contours of that debate, changed the way the questions were asked, and provided the answers. He wrote three autobiographies, each one adding to his story, as well as refining his ideas, arguments, and philosophies. These, along with his many speeches, newspaper editorials, and essays, helped persuade much of the public that slavery was wrong and must be ended. He didn't stop there, though. Once slavery was abolished, he continued to fight for equal rights for African Americans and for women. He worked for social justice until the very day of his death.

This statue of Frederick Douglass is located in Highland Park, in Rochester, New York.

This is the story of a man who was born in bondage, found his way to freedom, and became one of the greatest Americans in history.

CHAPTER ONE

The World of Bondage

We live in a time when African Americans own businesses, teach at colleges and universities, serve in Congress, sit on the highest court in the land, and can serve as president of the United States of America. Though African Americans still struggle for social and economic equality, it can be easy to forget the time when people of color not only had no rights but were considered property to be bought and sold like cattle. That's the way it was in the United States before the Civil War. To understand Frederick Douglass, first we have to understand the world he was born into and the one he helped to change.

Before the Civil War, slaves were bought and sold at auction much like farm equipment and animals. This illustration shows a slave auction.

Many Thousands Gone

In 1619, a Dutch ship pulled in at Jamestown, Virginia, and unloaded its cargo: twenty or so African men and women. These people had been captured, bound, and brought to North America to work on tobacco and rice plantations. For the next two hundred and some years, Africans like these would be stolen from their homes by slave traders, taken across the seas, and sold to Americans who forced them to work on their plantations. These people would be treated more like farm animals than people. They could be brutally beaten if they dared disobey or tried to escape. Families were often torn apart. Children could be taken away from their parents and sold to other slaveholders miles away. Married couples could similarly be separated. Slaves had little or no say in their circumstances, no control of their lives. Legally, they were property, and they were routinely treated far worse than most people today treat their pets.

In his autobiography *The Life and Times of Frederick Douglass*, Douglass describes very eloquently slavery's heartbreaking violence toward not only human bodies but human spirits:

> My mother and I were separated when I was but an infant—before I knew her as my mother. It is a common custom, in the part of Maryland from which I ran away, to part children from their mothers at a very early age. Frequently, before the child has reached its twelfth month, its mother is taken from it, and hired out on some farm a considerable distance off, and the child is placed under the care of an old woman, too old for field labor … I never saw my mother, to know her as such, more than four

> or five times in my life; and each of these times was very short in duration, and at night. She was hired by a Mr. Stewart, who lived about twelve miles [19 kilometers] from my home. She made her journeys to see me in the night, travelling the whole distance on foot, after the performance of her day's work. She was a field hand, and a whipping is the penalty of not being in the field at sunrise, unless a slave has special permission from his or her master to the contrary—a permission which they seldom get, and one that gives to him that gives it the proud name of being a kind master. I do not recollect of ever seeing my mother by the light of day. She was with me in the night. She would lie down with me, and get me to sleep, but long before I waked she was gone.[1]

Douglass also recalls in his memoirs seeing his relatives brutally beaten by their owner:

> He would at times seem to take great pleasure in whipping a slave. I have often been awakened at the dawn of day by the most heart-rending shrieks of an old aunt of mine, whom he used to tie up to a joist, and whip upon her naked back till she was literally covered with blood. No words, no tears, no prayers, from his gory victim, seemed to move his iron heart from its bloody purpose. The louder she screamed, the harder he whipped; and where the blood ran fastest, there he whipped longest. He would whip her to make her scream, and whip her to make her hush; and not until overcome by fatigue, would he cease to swing the blood-clotted cowskin.[2]

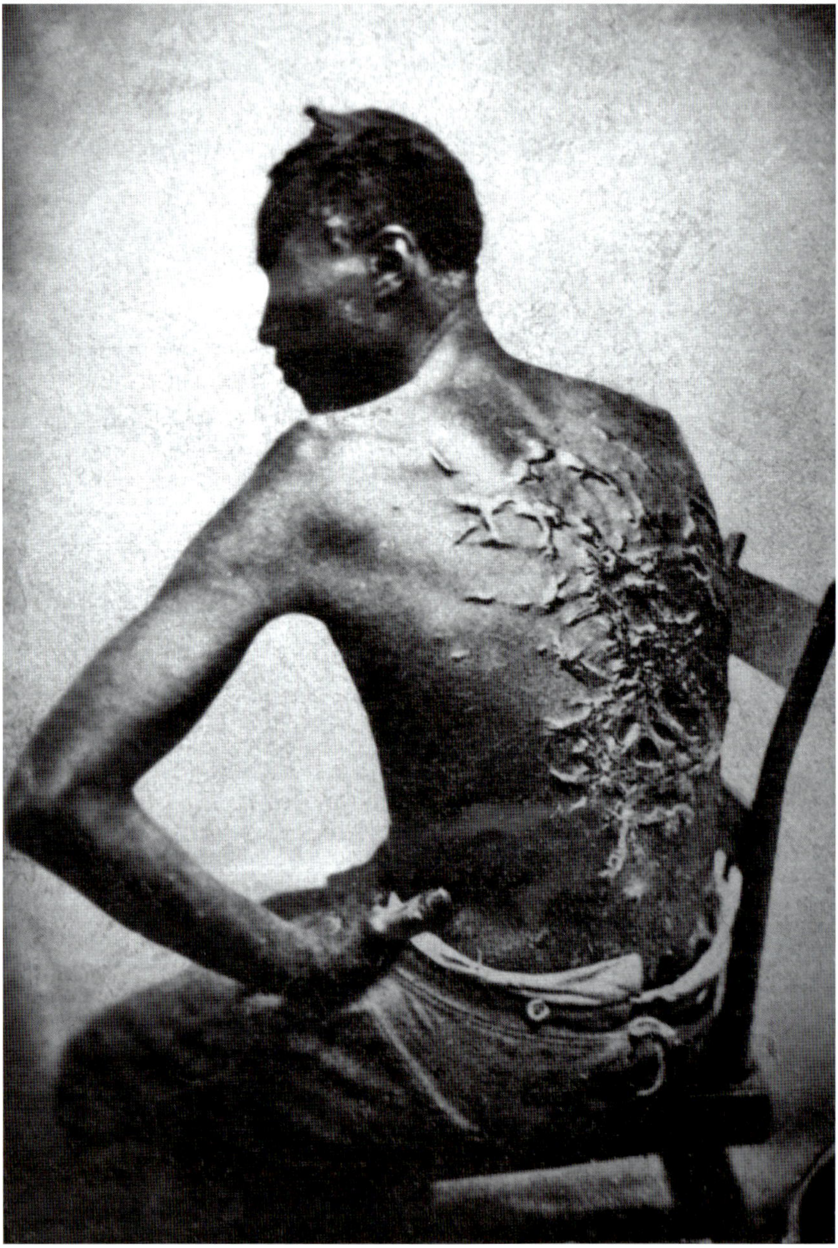

This photo was taken in April 1863. It shows Peter, a slave in Mississippi. He was left with these scars after being whipped by the overseer of the plantation where he worked. This happened to many slaves.

Whether or not a slave master actually took the whip to his slaves, the institution itself was violent—and it harmed not only its victims but its perpetrators. By dehumanizing slaves, slave owners became less human themselves. So what could have caused such a horrible institution to be accepted in a nation that had been founded on the principles of freedom and equality?

It Was About the Money

Like many injustices, the institution of slavery cannot be separated from economics. When the Declaration of Independence was signed in 1776, slavery was legal in all thirteen colonies. As slaves became less crucial to the economies in the Northern states, attitudes about slavery began to change. By the time the US Constitution was ratified in 1788, many Northern states had either already abolished slavery or were on the road to abolition. (Because of some states' gradual emancipation policies, by the mid-1800s, there were still quite a few slaves in Northern states. New York didn't reach full emancipation until the 1820s, and there were still slaves in New Jersey as late as 1850.) The Southern states, however, depended on slave labor to maintain their largely agricultural economies.

Slavery became a pivotal issue during the debate about the Constitution. In order to get the Southern slave states to ratify the new constitution, the Northern delegates—many of whom were hoping to see a quick end to slavery—gave in to several demands from the slave states. First, they agreed that no state could outlaw the slave trade for another twenty years. They also agreed that non-slave states had to return runaway slaves to their owners and that the federal government would step in to quell any slave uprisings. Perhaps most importantly, the new Constitution counted slaves, for purposes of congressional representation, as three-fifths of a person. This effectively gave the Southern states a great deal of legislative power they would not have had if only the free population had been counted. In 1790, the state with the most slaves was Virginia, and there, 44 percent of the population were slaves. About 60 percent of South Carolina's population were slaves, and across the Southern states combined, the percentage was near 40 percent. This would make it very difficult for the Northern states to pass any legislation that would limit slavery nationwide.

However, by the end of the eighteenth century, it looked as if slavery might die a natural death. The tobacco industry was in decline, and this removed one of the major economic reasons for slavery. Unfortunately, the "peculiar institution" (a common euphemism for slavery) was saved at the last minute when a young man named Eli Whitney invented the cotton gin, a machine that quickly and easily removes seeds from cotton fibers.

The English had mechanized the production of textiles and were in great need of cotton that was being grown in the southern United States. However, the crop was limited because it was very difficult to remove the seeds. The cotton gin made it feasible to grow many different types of cotton. It also completely reinvigorated the Southern economy based on cotton. The gin effectively removed the seeds, but alas, that's all it did. The production of cotton was still very labor intensive, so slave labor was once again an economic necessity in the South.

Even though slave labor was necessary to maintain the economy of the region, it took more than that to justify such a horrific practice. People who owned slaves or supported slavery were able to treat their fellow human beings in such an unspeakable way only by convincing themselves that these people weren't, in fact, fellow human beings. Even many people who saw blacks as fully human still thought that white people were superior to them—intellectually, morally, and in every other way. A correspondent of John C. Calhoun, South Carolina politician and staunch defender of slavery, wrote, "The Negro knows, acts and feels that God has put a mark of inferiority upon him."[3] It was a common view at the time, and not only among slave owners. Frederick Douglass would be instrumental in changing that view.

Let Them Tremble

Not everyone was accepting of slavery. Even at the time, some people saw it for the evil it was and worked hard—often at great personal risk—to bring it to an end. Some who advocated the end of slavery favored a gradual process. Others aimed only to contain slavery—keep it from spreading westward into new states as they were added to the Union. However, many in the abolitionist movement had a much more radical goal: they aimed to end slavery completely and immediately. In 1833, William Lloyd Garrison, a Massachusetts journalist, along with some sixty delegates, met in Philadelphia, Pennsylvania, to establish the American Anti-Slavery Society. The group was made up of people of all races and genders. It was dedicated to ending slavery using nonviolent means. It also condemned racial prejudice and advocated for full civil rights for blacks. Garrison was one of the most radical and vocal of the members. On January 1, 1831, in the first editorial of his antislavery newspaper the *Liberator*, Garrison had written, "Let Southern oppressors tremble; let their secret abettors tremble; let their Northern apologists tremble; let all the enemies of the persecuted blacks tremble."[4] He meant business. Now, with this new organization, the movement was organized and official.

Theirs was a difficult task, however. Even in the North, where slavery was largely illegal, outspoken denunciations of slavery were seldom appreciated. Helping runaway slaves was outright dangerous. Article IV, section 2 of the Constitution said, "No person held to service or labour in one state, under the laws thereof, escaping into another, shall, in consequence of any law or regulation therein, be discharged from such service or labour, but shall be delivered up on claim of the party to whom such service or labour may be due."[5] (This was later superseded by the Thirteenth Amendment.) Abolitionists in the North enacted laws designed to get around this, but Southern states continued to seek ways to more effectively enforce the clause. In 1850, Congress passed the Second Fugitive Slave Act, which was harsher than the previous one, and among other things, it imposed severe penalties on people who helped slaves escape.

Of course, this did not dampen the zeal of abolitionists like Garrison, but it did make their work more difficult. Over the next two decades, more abolitionist groups were formed, and more people joined the cause. Abolitionists continued to publicize the horrors of slavery and to convince both the public and elected officials of the moral necessity of bringing the practice to an immediate end.

Many prominent abolitionists were also active in the movement for women's rights. Lucretia Mott and Susan B. Anthony were two of many women's rights activists who worked in the abolition movement as well. Like Frederick Douglass, some abolitionists, such as Sojourner Truth, were former slaves.

SOJOURNER TRUTH

Sojourner Truth was called Isabella Baumfree when she was born a slave in New York. She was beaten and abused while in slavery. When she was nine years old, she was sold, along with a flock of sheep, for one hundred dollars. It is not known exactly when she was born, but in 1826, she escaped with her infant daughter. At least three of her other children had already been taken away from her and sold.

Once free, she changed her name to Sojourner Truth and worked hard for abolition. She was deeply religious and brought those values to the cause. Once, she heckled Frederick Douglass when he was giving a speech—calling him out for suggesting that abolishing slavery legally was hopeless, and that the only way out was by armed revolt.

During the Civil War she helped recruit black troops, and afterward she worked hard for the rights of free blacks. She was very critical of the abolitionist movement for focusing on rights for black men but not black women, and was a powerful voice for the women's movement.

Follow the Drinking Gourd

Meanwhile, others worked to free slaves before the institution itself was prohibited. Abolitionist groups were highly organized, with bylaws, membership rolls, meetings, and conventions. The Underground Railroad was something very different. It was actually neither a railroad nor was it literally underground. It was underground in the sense of being secret—very secret. The Underground Railroad was a loosely organized network of people who helped slaves escape and get to safety in Canada or to the North (which, because of the fugitive slave laws, was not as safe as Canada, where slavery had been against the law since 1834). The "stations" of the railroad were the homes, businesses—and often cellars, sheds, or barns—of people who were willing to hide escaped slaves for a night or two as they made their way north to freedom. The fugitive slaves were given food and clothing and a place to rest before they moved on to the next station.

Most of the workers on the Underground Railroad were African Americans, though many were white. "Conductors" of the railroad would go to a plantation, often disguised as slaves, to meet escaped slaves and help guide them out and to safety. A conductor would accompany a runaway slave to the next station, where the next conductor would take over. The first conductor would then return to retrieve another slave. According to one estimate, as many as one hundred thousand slaves escaped by way of the Underground Railroad between 1810 and 1850.

The instructions for how to find one's way to freedom were sometimes passed on in code, often in the form of songs that slaves would sing as they worked. The song "Follow the Drinking Gourd" is said to have been one such song. A

In the night sky, the Big Dipper (*star formation*) and the North Star (*top left star*) pointed the way to freedom for escaped slaves.

drinking gourd referred to the dipper people in the South used to scoop water from a well. In the song, it referred to the Big Dipper, the constellation used to locate the North Star, a guide for which way to go to find freedom.

One of the most famous members of the Underground Railroad was Harriet Tubman. Over the course of ten years, she made nineteen trips into the South and led three hundred slaves to freedom. Tubman was herself an escaped slave. In 1844, while still a slave, she married a free black man named John Tubman. In 1849, when she learned that she was soon to be sold, she left the planation on foot. Traveling at night and following the North Star, she made her way to Philadelphia, Pennsylvania. There she found work and earned enough money to go back for her family. She continued for a decade to take the huge risk of returning to slave territory to save others.

She was successful in part because she was clever. She tried to leave on Saturday nights because the notice of a runaway slave wouldn't be placed in the paper until Monday, giving them a day's head start. She carried a drug that would make babies sleep so that their cries wouldn't give away the group. She was incredibly compassionate, but also tough. She knew that if a runaway changed his or her mind and turned back, they would all be caught. She carried a gun, and if one of her charges started to turn back, she would threaten to shoot them, telling them that they would be free or die. She never killed anyone, though. She often bragged that in ten years and three hundred people, she never lost a soul. There was a $40,000 price on her head. Frederick Douglass wrote to Tubman in August 1868, saying, "Excepting John Brown—of sacred memory—I know of no one who has willingly encountered more perils and hardships to serve our enslaved people than you have."[6]

This portrait of Harriet Tubman was taken in 1868. She had worked long and hard to lead many escaped slaves to freedom.

Douglass himself made only one stop on the Underground Railroad for his escape, but he later served as a stationmaster on the railroad. Many others, whose names we will never know, worked in the dark and in secret to save others. These are some of the true heroes of our nation.

A Gathering Storm

By the mid-1850s, the nation was tearing itself apart over slavery. Pro- and antislavery forces were fighting in Kansas over whether the territory would enter the Union as a free or slave state. (Kansas entered the Union as a free state in 1861.) Abolitionist John Brown—the man mentioned in Douglass's letter to Tubman—had determined that a violent slave insurrection was the only hope for abolition. In October 1859, he led a group of dedicated followers in a raid on the US armory at Harpers Ferry, Virginia. He planned to use the weapons in a war to end slavery. He was caught, tried, convicted of treason, and hanged. Afterward, politicians worked to find a compromise to the slavery issue but couldn't come up with one.

In 1860, Abraham Lincoln was elected president. Though he did not favor immediate abolition, his election was the last straw for the Southern states. Seven states—South Carolina, Mississippi, Florida, Alabama, Georgia, Louisiana, and Texas—seceded from the United States and formed the Confederate States of America in response to Lincoln's election. Four other slave states—Virginia, Arkansas, North Carolina, and Tennessee—would soon follow. The institution of slavery had driven the country into what would become a very long and bloody civil war. This was the world that Frederick Douglass was born into, lived in, and ultimately changed.

This statue of Abraham Lincoln at the Lincoln Memorial in Washington, DC, watches over the nation he helped to preserve.

CHAPTER TWO

The Map to Freedom

Frederick Douglass was born a slave, but his life didn't take the same path as most slaves. In fact, it didn't follow a path of most people, free or slave. He was a remarkable man in many ways that go far beyond his daring escape from slavery. Like Harriet Tubman, when Douglass gained his freedom, he turned his attention to helping others get free. He did not do this by leading people one by one along the Underground Railroad. He did this by leading the entire nation along the road to a better, more civilized world.

This woodcut of Frederick Douglass shows him speaking to the public in England about the horrors of slavery and the need for abolition.

Keep Them Ignorant

Today we know that Frederick Douglass was born in Talbot County, Maryland, in 1818. Douglass, however, did not know that. He later wrote that for the most part, "slaves know as little of their ages as horses know of theirs, and it is the wish of most masters … to keep their slaves thus ignorant. I do not remember to have ever met a slave who could tell of his birthday."[1] Douglass's best guess was that he had been born in February 1817. After his mother was moved to a different plantation, young Frederick was cared for by his grandmother, Betsey Bailey, on Holmes Hill Farm. Douglass did not know who his father was but believed him to be white, and possibly Douglass's master. The fact that his father was white—and possibly his owner—made no difference at all. Douglass explained:

> Slavery had no recognition of fathers, and none of families. That the mother was a slave was enough for its deadly purpose. By law, the child followed the condition of its mother. The father might be a freeman and the child a slave … Father he might be, and not be husband, and could sell his own child without incurring reproach, if in its veins coursed one drop of African blood.[2]

When Douglass was around seven or eight years old, he was taken from his grandmother and sent to work in the Great House where the master of the plantation lived, a man named Colonel Edward Lloyd. Young Frederick had been happy living with his grandmother in her cabin. He played with the other children she cared for and fished in the mill pond. When he was delivered to the Great House, he felt abandoned and betrayed. Because he was too young to work in the fields, his new job was to bring in the cows each evening, chase chickens out of the garden, and run errands. Though the work was not too difficult, he was brokenhearted at being separated from his family. This was also the first time he witnessed the brutal treatment of his fellow slaves.

This enslaved African American family lived in a slave house much like the one Douglass lived in with his grandmother.

He didn't stay there long. About a year later, when he was around nine years old, Douglass was uprooted once again. This time he was given to a family in Baltimore, Maryland. His job was to be a companion for the family's little boy, Thomas. His new masters were Hugh and Sophia Auld. Frederick enjoyed looking after Thomas. But something happened in the Auld house that was to change the course of Douglass's life—and contribute greatly to changing the course of the nation.

ABCs

Up to this point, Douglass had lived in the country and had much enjoyed being out in nature. In Baltimore, though, he was mostly indoors or on hard city streets. However, Baltimore did provide one very special pleasure for the intelligent slave: reading. Sophia Auld was kind, gentle, and fond of Douglass at first. He later described her being very pious and spending a great deal of time reading the Bible out loud. This was the first time he had been exposed to reading, and he was very curious and wanted to learn to do it himself. He asked his mistress if she would teach him, and she agreed. He was an excellent pupil, very quickly learning the alphabet and a few simple words. Sophia was delighted with his progress. Her husband was not.

When Sophia proudly told Hugh Auld of Douglass's progress, her husband was very much displeased. The couple got into an argument about it, and Douglass overheard the whole thing. Hugh explained to his wife exactly what the slave system was like. Sophia was treating young Frederick as if he were a child, but in fact, according to Hugh, he was no more than property, and it was essential that this human property not be taught to read. Reading made slaves desire their freedom, and learning made them unfit for the work slaves were expected to do. Slaves were meant to know nothing more than what they were instructed to do by their masters. Hugh Auld forbade his wife to continue Douglass's reading lessons. (At that time women were subject to the will of their husbands, so she had no more choice in the matter than Douglass did.)

Fortunately, once the spark of learning had been lit in the child's mind, it was not easily put out. Exposure to reading had a powerful effect on Douglass. However, the lecture he overheard about the system of slavery may have had an even more profound effect. Though Hugh didn't realize it, he was giving his young slave the road map to freedom. Douglass realized immediately that knowledge was the key to freedom. Later, he would write:

> This was a new and special revelation, dispelling a painful mystery against which my youthful understanding had struggled, and struggled in vain, to wit, the white man's power to perpetuate the enslavement of the black man. "Very well," thought I. "Knowledge unfits a child to be a slave." I instinctively assented to the proposition, and from that moment I understood the direct pathway from slavery to freedom.[3]

Unbreakable

Sophia had been convinced by her husband's arguments and made every effort to keep Douglass from reading. If she saw him with a book or newspaper, she jerked it away from him. Whenever he was alone or away from the family for more

This drawing shows the city of Baltimore, Maryland, as it looked circa 1828, when Frederick Douglass lived there working for the Auld family. He missed the countryside, but he discovered the joy of books.

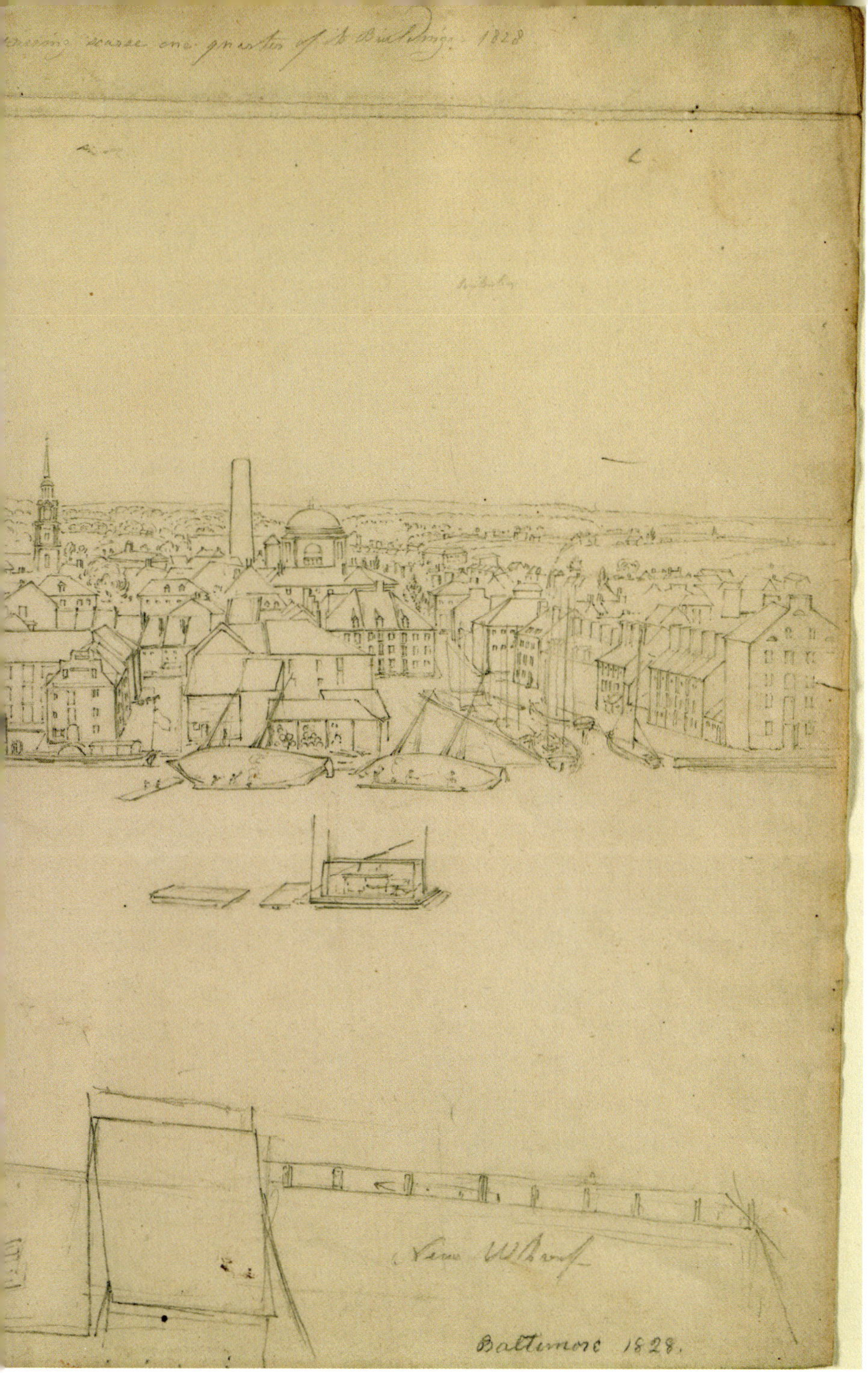

New Wharf
Baltimore 1828.

than a few minutes, he was suspected of reading and called in to explain what he had been doing. Nevertheless, Douglass carried on his reading lessons on his own.

Now that he was living in Baltimore, he was around more white children. He persuaded some of them to share their school lessons with him and teach him what they learned in school. Soon he could read and write quite well.

When Douglass was around the age of fifteen, owing to several deaths and complications of inheritance among the family that owned him, he was moved to a new master, this one in St. Michaels in Talbot County. His new master found Douglass to be a less than suitable slave and rented him out to a man named Edward Covey. Covey was a slave-breaker—a man who worked slaves incredibly hard and treated them brutally in order to obliterate any sense of rebellion or even humanity they might have still retained. Covey beat Douglass almost daily—until one day when Douglass fought back. Douglass was strong and powerful even in his teens and easily bested his cruel master. The beatings stopped, and not long after, Covey passed Douglass on to another slave renter. This man was a kinder master, and while working there, Douglass began a secret slave school in the house of a free black man. There, Douglass taught as many as forty other slaves to read.

During all this time, Douglass had been planning to escape. He was sent back to Baltimore to work for his master's brother. Once there, he was rented out to work on Baltimore's docks. He learned a trade as a ship's caulker. He often worked alongside white people or free blacks. He certainly had more freedom than he had on the plantation, but the experience just made him yearn more for freedom. He wrote, "The kindness of the slavemaster only gilds the chain of slavery, and detracts nothing from its weight or power."[4]

Anna Murray Douglass was the first wife of Frederick Douglass.

Freedom

During this time, Douglass met and fell in love with a free black woman named Anna Murray. Of course, being slave and free, they were not allowed to marry. However, Douglass had a plan.

The authorities were always on the lookout for runaway slaves. Free blacks were required to carry papers at all times. These papers proved that they were free. A black person could not board a train or a boat without them. In order to escape to a free state in the North, Douglass would have to have papers. The papers were quite specific. They included not only a general description of the holder, but details about specific scars and other marks that might identify him. Often free blacks would loan their papers to slaves, who would use them to escape, and then send the papers back when they got to a free state where papers were not required. This was a problem for Douglass because he was such a distinctive-looking man. Even at just twenty years old, he was tall and well built.

A friend of his who was a sailor loaned him his papers. The description wasn't too good, but Douglass was willing to take the risk. He dressed in a sailor's uniform and boarded a train. The train left Maryland and passed through Delaware, another slave state, before coming to the ferry at the Susquehanna River. He crossed into Pennsylvania, a free state. When he reached Philadelphia, he waited until night, then took another train to New York. In just under twenty-four hours, he had made the dangerous journey from slavery to freedom.

When he arrived in New York, in September 1838, he encountered a sailor who took him to the home of David Ruggles. Ruggles was an African American member of the Underground Railroad. Douglass immediately wrote to Anna

Murray, and she joined him in New York. Ruggles quickly rounded up a minister, and Douglass and Murray were married in his home. The next morning the couple left for New Bedford, Massachusetts, a whaling town, where Douglass hoped to find work using his skill as a ship caulker.

No Slavery but Plenty of Prejudice

In Baltimore, Douglass had gone by the name Frederick Bailey (having long since dropped his two middle names, Augustus Washington). His false papers identified him as Stanley. When he reached New York, he changed his name to Frederick Johnson. This was necessary because even though he was no longer in a slave state, he was technically still a slave—a runaway slave. If he were identified and caught, he would almost certainly be returned to his master. (The 1850 Fugitive Slave Act, which would increase penalties against people who helped runaway slaves, had not yet been passed, but a similar act from 1793 was in force.) In New Bedford, it turned out there were many people named Johnson, so to reduce the chances of confusion (and possibly awkward questions about relatives), Douglass changed his name yet again.

A man named Nathan Johnson had been helping the young couple get settled. Douglass asked him to choose a name. His only requirement was that he keep his first name, Frederick—he wanted to keep that much of his own identity. Johnson had been reading the poem "The Lady of the Lake" by Sir Walter Scott and chose the name one of the characters, Douglass (though the character in the poem has only one *s*). It seems fitting that a man who was inspired to freedom by a love of reading should take the name of a character from a poem.

This was the home of Nathan and Mary Johnson, the black family who sheltered Frederick Douglass when he first arrived in New Bedford, Massachusetts.

New Bedford did not turn out to be as welcoming a place as Douglass and his wife had hoped. There was plenty of work on the docks, but Douglass soon learned that even in the free states, prejudice against blacks was strong. White tradesmen refused to work alongside a black man. He ended up having to take odd jobs to support himself and Anna. Eventually, he found work in a factory.

On the other hand, their new home offered some pleasant surprises. Douglass was astonished to find how good the living conditions in the North were. He had expected that, lacking slaves, the people in the North would be poor, like Southern whites who were not slave owners. "I saw few or no dilapidated houses, with poverty-stricken inmates; no half-naked children and barefooted women, such as I had been accustomed to see in Hillsborough, Easton, St. Michael's, and Baltimore," he noted.[5] He was also pleasantly surprised at the condition of the black community he found there:

> But the most astonishing as well as the most interesting thing to me was the condition of the colored people, a great many of whom, like myself, had escaped thither as a refuge from the hunters of men. I found many, who had not been seven years out of their chains, living in finer houses, and evidently enjoying more of the comforts of life, than the average of slaveholders in Maryland ... I found the colored people much more spirited than I had supposed they would be. I found among them a determination to protect each other from the bloodthirsty kidnapper, at all hazards.[6]

LIFE OF THE FREE

Though blacks were free in the Northern states, they still had many problems to overcome. They were rarely allowed to vote or serve on juries. Housing, transportation, and education were segregated. Blacks often had difficulty finding good jobs. And of course, those who were escaped slaves had to be vigilant about avoiding capture.

Amazingly, not all freed blacks moved North. Many stayed in the South. In fact, by the beginning of the Civil War, there were more free blacks in the Confederate states than in the Northern states. Not all free blacks in the South were former slaves who had been freed, of course. Some were immigrants from places like the West Indies. (And some of these immigrants were slave owners themselves.) Other free blacks had been folded into the United States when the country bought a vast territory, called the Louisiana Purchase, from France, in 1803.

In the South, most free blacks lived in cities, far from the plantations that enslaved their fellow blacks. More of them were female than male. It was much easier for a man to travel the often great distances to the North, so women were more likely to stay down South and get jobs doing housework for white people in the cities. However, whether they lived in the South or the North, blacks endured a great deal of abuse and discrimination, even when they were free.

Another thing he discovered in New Bedford was that these black people and a great many white people were committed not only to protecting each other from the "blood-thirsty kidnapper" but to ending the institution of slavery altogether.

Soul on Fire

Once Douglass and Anna had settled into their new home, they subscribed to abolitionist newspaper the *Liberator*, which was being published in nearby Boston. The motto that appeared in the *Liberator*'s very first edition had boldly proclaimed, "Our country is the world—our countrymen are mankind."[7] The editor of the newspaper, William Lloyd Garrison, was not a timid man. In the very first issue of the paper, he responded to people who favored a gradual and moderate approach to ending slavery: "Urge me not to use moderation in a cause like the present. I am in earnest—I will not equivocate—I will not excuse—I will not retreat a single inch—AND I WILL BE HEARD."[8]

Douglass had known many slaves who were passionate about gaining their freedom, but they could not speak out about their condition. Likewise, he had met people who worked with the Underground Railroad and necessarily had to be very quiet about what they did. When he picked up the *Liberator*, for the first time he encountered people who were speaking out with loud voices and demanding an end to slavery. The effect on Douglass was electrifying. Later, he wrote, "The paper became my meat and my drink. My soul was set all on fire. Its sympathy for my brethren in bonds—its scathing denunciations of slaveholders—its faithful exposures of slavery—and its powerful attacks upon the upholders of the institution—sent a thrill of joy through my soul, such as I had never felt before!"[9]

This drawing shows an antislavery meeting on the Boston Commons in 1835. Many white abolitionists attended, as did a few free blacks.

Soon Douglass began attending local antislavery meetings. He generally did not speak much at the meetings because he felt that other people were saying well enough what he believed. Also, he recalled that at that time he had not yet lost some of the habits of being a slave and found it difficult to speak before white people. But on August 11, 1841, he did say a few words at an antislavery meeting on Nantucket. It was easier than he had expected. In fact, he was a natural speaker. From that day on, his was a powerful voice on behalf of his fellow slaves, fellow African Americans, and fellow human beings of all kinds.

The people who heard Douglass speak that day (and on many other days to come) responded not unlike Douglass had when he first read the *Liberator*. He set souls on fire. One of the books Douglass had been able to get his hands on during his days as a slave in Baltimore was *The Columbian Orator*. It was a collection of political essays and speeches. Douglass studied the book carefully. He absorbed the style of making an argument as well as presenting one. He read the book aloud and practiced delivering the speeches. This skill with rhetoric, combined with his natural, rich baritone voice, made him a persuasive and powerful speaker. That wasn't the only thing that impressed his fellow abolitionists. His first-person account of life as a slave was jolting and further inspired people to work hard to eliminate slavery.

In 1841, the Massachusetts Anti-Slavery Society recruited Douglass to go on a public speaking tour. He did so, and was a popular and effective speaker on the circuit. John Collins, a leader of the Massachusetts Anti-Slavery Society, often introduced Douglass to an audience by saying that Douglass was "a graduate from the peculiar institution, with [his] diploma written on his back."[10]

After a time, people began to doubt that Douglass had really been a slave. He was too well educated and articulate, it seemed. Douglass could not give the details needed to prove his case, however. If he had been identified, his master could demand his return. He carefully avoided mentioning his real name, the name of his masters, or the state or county he came from. Even so, it was a great risk for Douglass to become so public a figure. This, of course, only supported claims that he was an imposter.

In 1845, after the urging of some friends, he decided to put his entire story—names and places included—on paper. As it turned out, Douglass was not only a great speaker, but he was a great writer as well. His autobiography (the first of three that he would write) was a brief but powerful book called *Narrative of the Life of Frederick Douglass, an American Slave*. It is a fascinating read even today. Its unflinching portrayal of the realities of slavery is every bit as moving and disturbing as it was in 1845. The book had proved Douglass was who he said he was, but it also told his owner where he could be found. Douglass was sure he was safe as long as he was in public—he had many friends who were willing to take great risks to prevent his capture—but there was always the possibility that he would be grabbed at a time when no friends were around to protect him. In order to be safe from capture, Douglass left the United States for England, where slavery was illegal.

Douglass enjoyed his time in England and made many friends there. A group of them, including several members of the Society of Friends (a religious group also known as Quakers, who were active in the abolition movement in the United States as well), came up with a plan for securing Douglass's freedom so he could return to his home. They raised the money and bought his freedom from his current owner, Hugh Auld. They presented Douglass with his manumission, or emancipation, papers. He was now a free man, who could travel where he pleased without fear of being captured and returned to slavery.

Douglass was grateful, because even though he could have stayed in England and brought his family to join him, he felt strongly that it was his duty to return to the United States, where he could work to free other oppressed people in his native land.

Home and Free

Douglass returned home as a free man—but not an equal one. The ship he traveled on (both to and from England) would not allow him to book a cabin. He had to travel in steerage, where people who could not afford a cabin were housed. Nor was he allowed to enter the ship's dining room. This seemed a small matter after having spent his first twenty years in slavery. However, he was not unaware that such discrimination was wrong and needed to be addressed.

Douglass worked for the abolition of slavery up to the very day the cruel institution was finally outlawed by the Thirteenth Amendment to the Constitution in 1865. During the Civil War, he worked for the government recruiting black Americans to fight in the Union Army. He met with President Lincoln and encouraged him to enlist black soldiers in the Union Army and treat them as equals of the other soldiers. Throughout the Civil War, he insisted and continually reminded the nation's leaders that this was a war not just to keep the nation together, but one to end slavery once and for all.

Abolishing slavery was not his only goal. He also worked—both before and after abolition—for social, political, and economic equality for African Americans. His concern for civil rights was not limited to people like himself. He was also very active in the movement for voting rights and other rights for women. After the war, he became the de facto leader of the African American community, advising and supporting them in the difficult days after emancipation. Later in life, he continued to serve his country in several government positions. In 1889, President Benjamin Harrison appointed Douglass consul general to Haiti.

Anna died in 1882, and a few years later, Douglass remarried. His second wife, Helen, was white. This caused some controversy in a nation that had ended slavery but still not worked out its many issues surrounding race. But Douglass and his new wife did not let this interfere with their happiness. Douglass died in 1895 after returning home from a meeting of the National Council of Women.

CHAPTER THREE

A Lamentable Schism

The abolition movement was a powerful movement, but as in most organizations, its members sometimes disagreed or developed rivalries. That would be the case between Douglass and his first mentor, William Lloyd Garrison. Initially, Garrison's newspaper inspired Douglass, and so did the man himself. They shared a passion to end slavery and worked together toward that end. Frederick Douglass became one of the nation's most influential black abolitionists. Garrison became one of the most influential white abolitionists. However, eventually their relationship

This portrait shows abolitionist and writer William Lloyd Garrison.

would be challenged over basic differences about abolition, the cause that initially united them.

The Impatient Pacifist

Garrison was born in 1805 in Newburyport, Massachusetts. His father deserted the family when Garrison was still a child. Young William had to work at odd jobs, such as selling molasses or gathering firewood, to earn money for food. Eventually, he began to work as a newspaper writer and editor. When he was a young man, he became an abolitionist. In January 1831, he began publishing a newspaper dedicated to articles and essays promoting the cause of abolition. Every week without fail for thirty-five years, Garrison put out an issue of the *Liberator*. The newspaper would be in publication until the end of the Civil War, when its work was no longer needed. In the last issue, Garrison wrote, "My vocation as an abolitionist is ended."[1] He was no doubt both proud and relieved.

Garrison differed with many abolitionists at the time in that he favored immediate and complete abolition—and not only abolition. He believed that black people—and not just free blacks, but former slaves as well—should be given all the rights and respect of their fellow white citizens. Many people at the time thought that slavery should be ended, but gradually. They worried that freeing so many blacks at once would have dire economic and social consequences. Assimilating four million free blacks into American society would take some careful thought and planning, many thought. Garrison, however, saw the issue not as an economic or political issue so much as a moral one. Slavery was, according to Garrison, a national sin that must be repented. Douglass immediately recognized Garrison's religious belief as well as the passion of his heart in the matter of slavery. In his second autobiography, *My Bondage and My Freedom*, Douglass wrote that Garrison believed "prejudice against color was rebellion against God. Of all men beneath the sky, the slaves, because most neglected and despised, were nearest and dearest to his great heart."[2]

Garrison founded the American Anti-Slavery Society, but many of his views were extreme at the time, even to those who supported immediate and complete emancipation. At one point, he advocated a peaceful secession of the free Northern states from the slaveholding Southern states, believing that the nation could not exist with any slaveholding states as a part of it. He was also opposed to political activism. This was useless, he thought, because politics required too many compromises. Garrison was not a man who was patient with compromise. He was, however, very much a pacifist.

Garrison also supported equal rights for women and insisted on allowing them full membership in the society. These views and others caused splits within the movement. Conservatives who did not like the inclusion of women formed a separate group, and those who believed that political action could end slavery began a political party of their own. If Garrison's extreme views diluted his influence within the organizations of the abolitionist movement, they only increased the influence of his writings.

Garrison's views were, for the most part, very consistent with those of his friend Frederick Douglass. Douglass, too, favored immediate and complete emancipation, saw it as a moral issue rather than a purely political one, and supported equal rights as well as freedom for blacks. He also supported equal rights for women. However, after many years of working side by side for the cause and developing a deep friendship, the relationship between the two great abolitionist leaders began to fray.

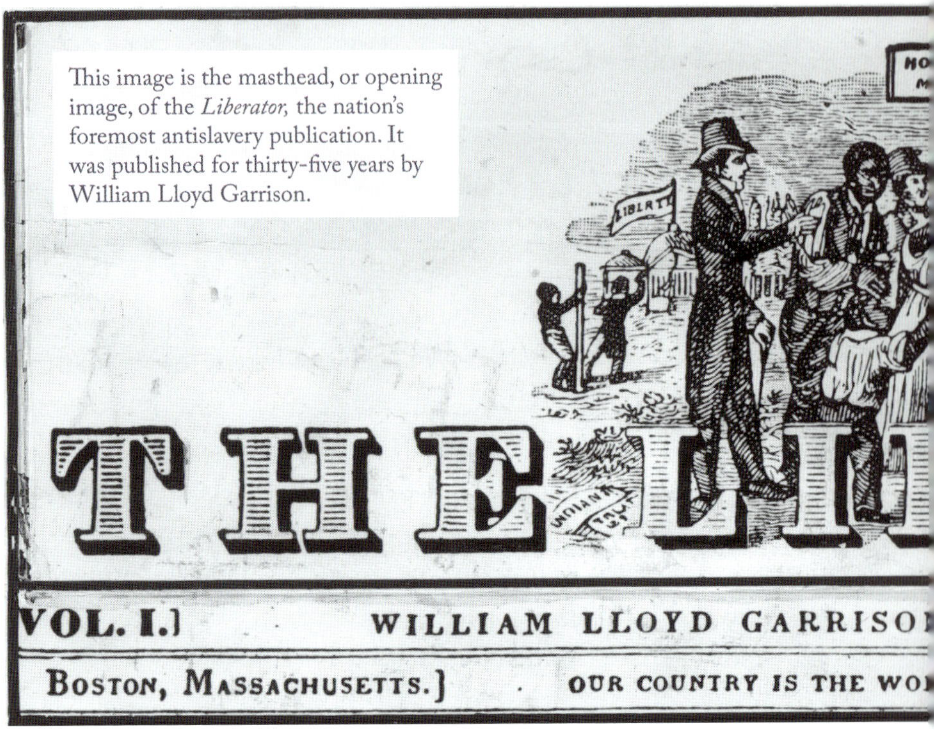

This image is the masthead, or opening image, of the *Liberator,* the nation's foremost antislavery publication. It was published for thirty-five years by William Lloyd Garrison.

Far More to Say

In 1847, Douglass and his family moved from New Bedford, Massachusetts, to Rochester, New York, where Douglass began publishing his own abolitionist weekly, called the *North Star*. The paper was so named because escaped slaves would follow the North Star to find their way to freedom. In addition to advocating for abolition, the *North Star* often carried articles about how former slaves could improve themselves socially and intellectually.

Launching his own paper gave Douglass the opportunity to distance himself from Garrison and the American Anti-Slavery Society. He now had his own business and source of income, so

could express himself freely even if he disagreed with his fellow abolitionists. It also gave Douglass a place where he could speak with his own voice.

Garrison and others in his movement—often called Garrisonians—encouraged Douglass to speak at abolition meetings and give public lectures sharing the story of his life as a slave. This had a powerful effect on listeners, many of whom were astonished that a slave could express himself at all, much less so eloquently. But after a few years of this, Douglass had far more to say. He wanted a forum in which he could speak his mind without having his words scripted by the Garrisonians. Later Douglass wrote of his years on the lecture circuit with the American Anti-Slavery Society: "'Tell your story, Frederick,'

JOHN BROWN'S BODY

Another point of disagreement between Douglass and Garrison was Douglass's support for John Brown. Brown was a ferocious abolitionist. He was every bit as committed to the abolition of slavery as was Garrison. However, where Garrison was a pacifist, Brown was more than willing, even eager, to fight for the cause.

In his life, Brown lived in many places around the North and worked at a variety of jobs. He was a farmer, a merchant, and a land speculator, and was not successful at any of these. His true passion was ending slavery. He was a member of the Underground Railroad and gave free land to escaped slaves.

By 1847, Brown had come up with a plan to begin a war to free the slaves, and he put this plan into action in Kansas in 1855. He led a group of fighters in attacks on proslavery towns. He killed several people. Then he decided to take his war east. He would need supplies for his army, and to that end, in 1859 he led twenty-one men, mostly white, in an attack on a federal armory in Harpers Ferry, Virginia. The raid was a failure, and Brown was caught and hanged.

Douglass had mixed feelings about Brown. Obviously he agreed with Brown's basic position and was himself increasingly leaning to a more radical and violent solution to the problem of slavery. He communicated with Brown, and even let Brown stay in his house for several months. However, when Brown asked Douglass to join him in the Harpers Ferry raid, Douglass declined. Douglass was willing to go quite far to free slaves, but he could see no good coming from the plan to attack the government arsenal. While he admired Brown's passion, he did not trust his leadership or his strategic ability.

When Brown was caught, he had a letter from Douglass in his possession. Another man caught in the raid denounced Douglass for not getting involved with the raid after supposedly promising to do so. That could have been

Antislavery activist John Brown embraced violence in the interest of ending slavery. His plans were not successful, however.

enough to get Douglass arrested as co-conspirator. He left for England for a time, on a trip already organized, but one that had another meaning to Douglass, who was now escaping an arrest warrant.

Though he tried very hard, Brown did not achieve much in the way of ending slavery while he was alive. However, as a martyr to the cause, his name was quite useful to the movement after he was dead. A song called "John Brown's Body," originally about an unknown soldier but later rewritten to define the legendary man, became a popular marching song for abolitionists.

would whisper my then revered friend, William Lloyd Garrison, as I stepped upon the platform. I could not always obey, for I was now reading and thinking. New views of the subject were presented to my mind. It did not entirely satisfy me to narrate wrongs; I felt like *denouncing* them."[3]

Garrison was not pleased with Douglass's move away from the society, though it is difficult to say exactly why. He was a great supporter of black enterprise, so it is doubtful that his reaction had anything to do with some kind of hidden racism, though some commentators have suggested that it did. (Garrison and others in his movement do seem to have treated Douglass with some paternalism and condescension. However, that explains Douglass's desire to strike out on his own more than Garrison's reasons for being offended.) More likely, Garrison was offended that his protégé would go into direct competition with him. There were several other abolitionist papers at this time, but the *North Star* was the one that was a serious rival to the *Liberator*. Even this, however, doesn't seem to quite explain Garrison's antipathy.

While Garrison was devoted to his paper, his devotion was only because it helped with the cause that was close to his heart. The *Liberator* was never a financial success, and in any case, Garrison gave most of the profits to the movement. He was relatively poor his entire life and did not seem to have any ambition beyond the achievement of social justice. In any case, however Garrison felt about the *North Star* personally, he spoke highly of it in print, and gave it excellent reviews in his own paper. More likely Garrison's reaction to Douglass's venture into publishing was an early indication of the gulf between the two men that was beginning to develop over more substantial differences.

Garrison (as well as many other abolitionists) was philosophically opposed to paying slave owners to free slaves.

Even when the ultimate intention was to free a person, paying a slave owner for a slave seemed a tacit endorsement of slavery, and made the buyer a part of the noxious institution. It also economically rewarded people who traded in slaves. Douglass, of course, had been freed only when friends raised the money and bought his freedom. He called it "blood money" and said:

> Some of my uncompromising antislavery friends in this country failed to see the wisdom of this commercial transaction, and were not pleased that I consented to it, even by my silence. They thought it a violation of antislavery principles, conceding the right of property in man, and a wasteful expenditure of money. For myself, viewing it simply in the light of a ransom, or as money extorted by a robber, and my liberty of more value than one hundred and fifty pounds sterling [$23,000 in 2018], I could not see either a violation of the laws of morality or of economy.[4]

Garrison was also opposed to working within the system. At times he sounded as if he were almost an anarchist. He opposed any kind of political involvement and did not believe in running antislavery candidates for public office, or even in voting. Douglass had at first seemed to agree with this. But the passage in 1850 of the newer, more severe Fugitive Slave Act changed his mind. By 1851, he was advocating voting as a powerful means of changing policy and eventually outlawing slavery.

Douglass and Garrison also had deep disagreements about the US Constitution. The document had been a masterwork of compromise. In order to get the slave states to ratify it in the late 1700s, delegates from the non-slave states had made

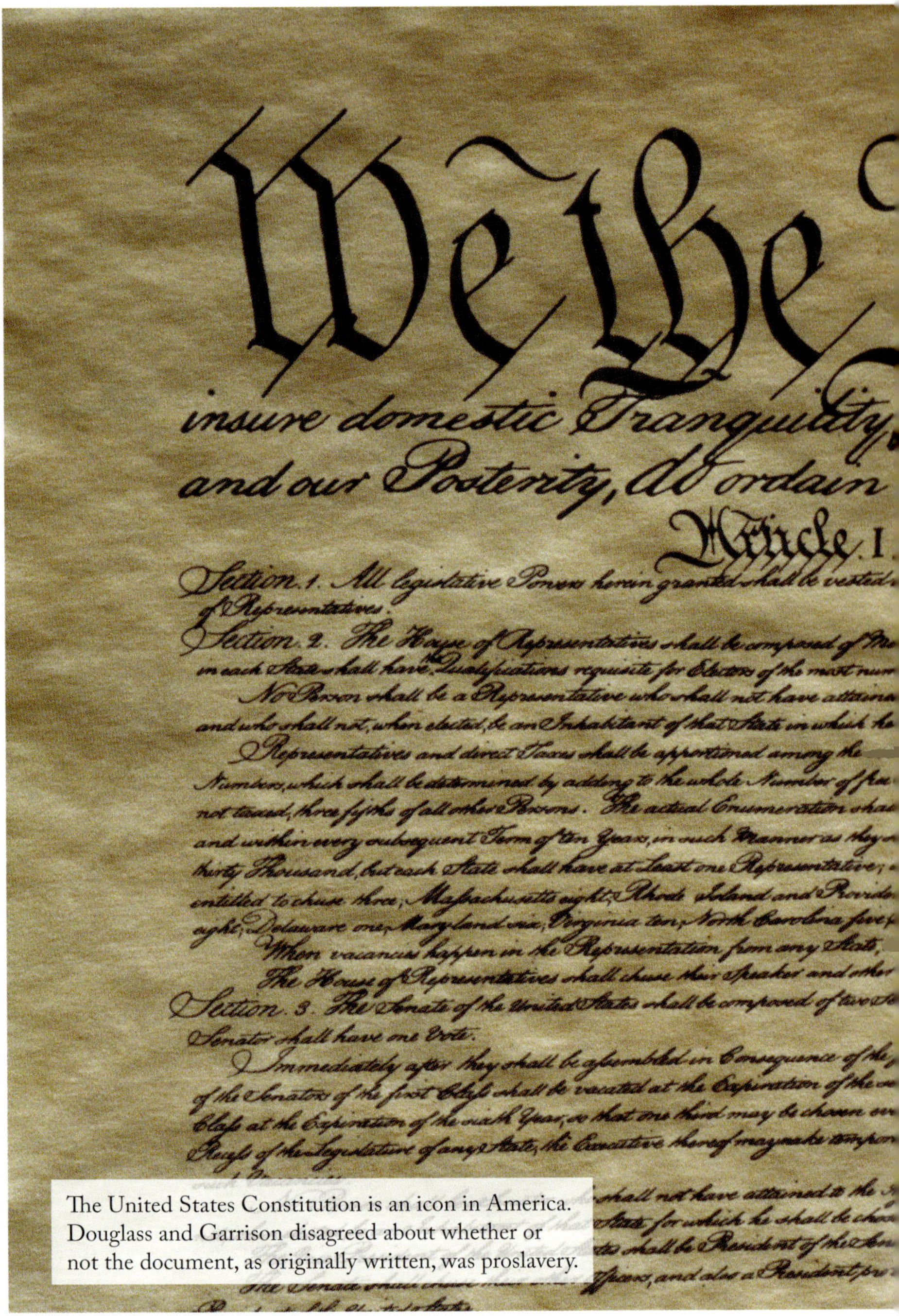

The United States Constitution is an icon in America. Douglass and Garrison disagreed about whether or not the document, as originally written, was proslavery.

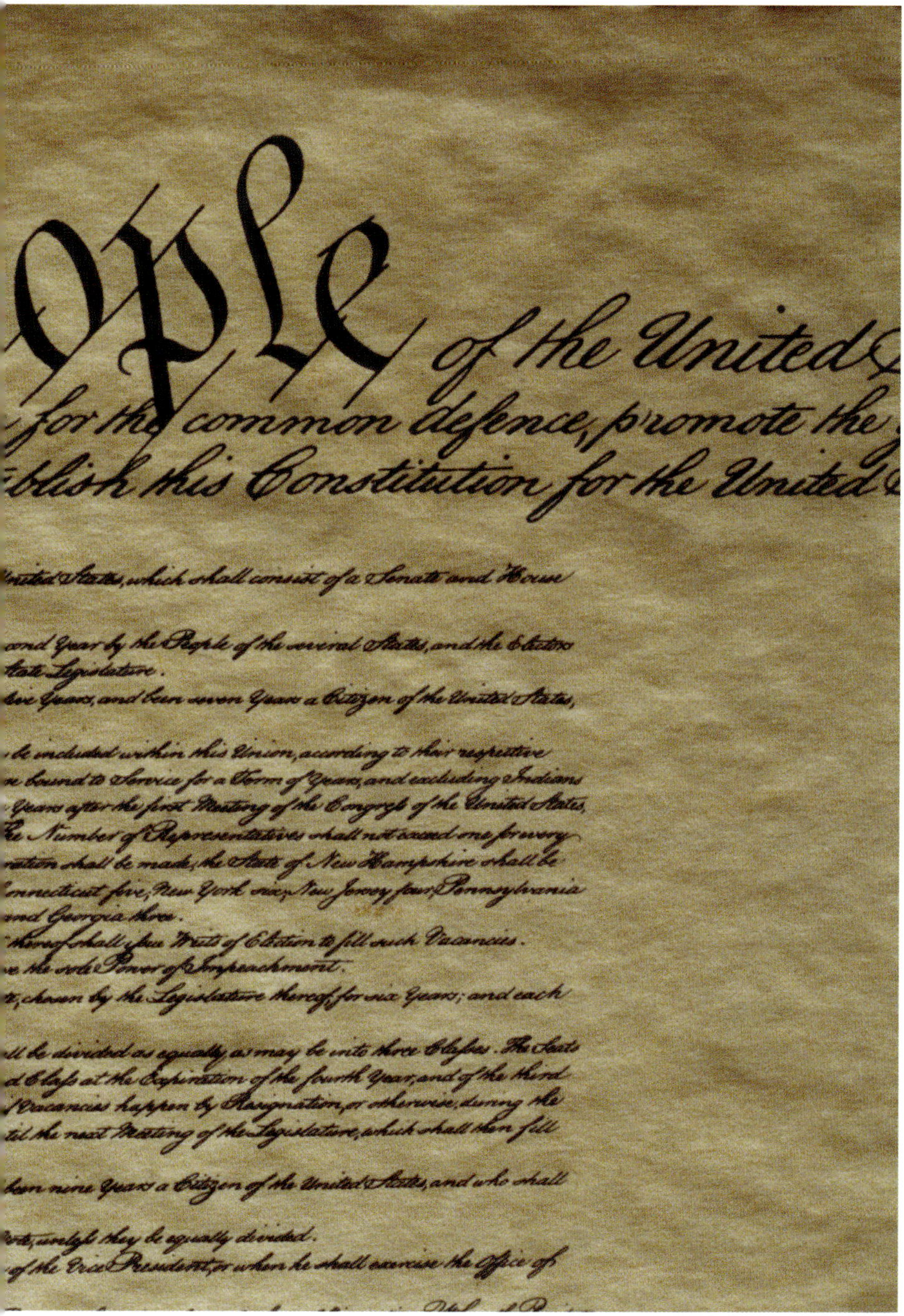
ople of the United
for the common defence, promote the
blish this Constitution for the United

a number of concessions at the Constitutional Convention. Among these were the three-fifths clause, which counted a slave as three-fifths of a person for purposes of representation. This gave slave states more power in the legislature than they would have had had only free citizens been counted. The document also included language requiring citizens in free states to return runaway slaves and required the federal government to help quell slave insurrections. Garrison considered the Constitution a proslavery document. He believed that in order to establish a nation without slavery, the Constitution would have to be scrapped and a new one written. By 1842, Garrison and some of his supporters were suggesting "disunion" of the Northern states from the Southern states. At a Fourth of July picnic in 1854, Garrison pulled a particularly outlandish stunt. He publicly burned a copy of the US Constitution.

Douglass disagreed with Garrison's views of the Constitution. He believed that the founding document was not inherently proslavery, and that its commitment to equality and self-government could be understood to extend to all people. In fact, he argued, the Constitution might well be one of the strongest tools in the hands of abolitionists. Garrison called the Constitution "a covenant with death and an agreement with Hell."[5] Douglass saw it somewhat differently. In 1860, in a speech to an abolitionist group in Glasgow, Scotland, he carefully outlined his views on the Constitution: "The Constitution may be right, the Government is wrong. If the Government has been governed by mean, sordid, and wicked passions, it does not follow that the Constitution is mean, sordid, and wicked." He went on to denounce the views of the Garrisonians and explain his differing view: "I, on the other hand, deny that the Constitution guarantees the right to hold property in man, and believe that the way to abolish slavery in America is to vote such men into power as will use their powers for the abolition of slavery."[6] Douglass not only explained that the Constitution could be used to abolish slavery, but he explained how:

> I would act for the abolition of slavery through the Government—not over its ruins ... If the South has made the Constitution bend to the purposes of slavery, let the North now make that instrument bend to the cause of freedom and justice ... Now let the freemen of the North, who have the power in their own hands, and who can make the American Government just what they think fit, resolve to blot out for ever the foul and haggard crime, which is the blight and mildew, the curse and the disgrace of the whole United States.[7]

In other words, if a nation founded in and operated by democratic principles had supported slavery, that same nation could reverse course and democratically abolish it.

The rift between the two men was deep and not easily mended. Garrison wrote in a letter to a friend, "With Douglass, the die seems to be cast. I lament the schism, but it is unavoidable."[8] They would be estranged throughout the war years. Mutual friend and fellow abolitionist Harriet Beecher Stowe tried to reconcile the old friends, but it would be many years before they were at peace with one another once more.

As Douglass's views changed—and his experiences deepened—he continued to write his story. His three autobiographies show the nuances of his views on how slavery ought to be abolished, and what kind of society should replace it.

Frederick Douglass

NARRATIVE

OF THE

LIFE

OF

FREDERICK DOUGLASS,

AN

AMERICAN SLAVE.

WRITTEN BY HIMSELF.

BOSTON:
PUBLISHED AT THE ANTI-SLAVERY OFFICE,
No. 25 CORNHILL.
1845.

CHAPTER FOUR

Telling and Retelling the Story

Over the course of his life, Frederick Douglass wrote three separate autobiographies. Each one told and expanded on his story, adding details to existing text, as well as adding parts of his biography that had not yet happened when he wrote the earlier volumes. The books differ from each other in more ways as well, particularly in the political and philosophical approach Douglass took to his subject matter. A close look at how Douglass's writing evolved over the years gives interesting insight into not only Douglass himself but to the world in which he lived.

This is the title page of the first edition of *Narrative of the Life of Frederick Douglass, an American Slave.*

How Mankind Ought to Treat Each Other

Douglass's first biography, *Narrative of the Life of Frederick Douglass, an American Slave*, was much like the talks Garrison urged him to give on the lecture circuit. He told his story. The *Narrative* was an exposé of slavery, intended to awaken people in the free states to the realities of the "peculiar institution." It was an intense portrayal of slave society. Even today, it can be difficult to read. It was effective too. Though Douglass's speeches and lectures had the same effect, the book provided additional details to document that Douglass really had spent his first twenty years as a slave. Garrison wrote a preface to the book, and the front matter of the book also included a letter vouching for its author, this one from Wendell Phillips, another prominent abolitionist. In the letter, Phillips wrote to Douglass, "You remember the old fable of 'The Man and the Lion,' where the lion complained that he should not be so misrepresented 'when lions wrote history.' I am glad the time has come when the 'lions write history.'" Then Phillips goes on to praise Douglass and his work, and to say, "We have known you long, and can put the most entire confidence in your truth, candor, and sincerity."[1] For his part, Garrison tells the story of how he came to know Douglass, and then clearly states the purpose of Douglass's message:

> He who can peruse [the book] without a tearful eye, a heaving breast, an afflicted spirit,—without being filled with an unutterable abhorrence of slavery and all its abettors, and animated with a determination to seek the immediate overthrow of that execrable system,—without trembling for the fate of this country in the hands of a righteous God … must have a flinty heart.[2]

The book did indeed soften many hearts. People who might not have had the opportunity to or even an interest in hearing Douglass speak read the book and were moved—often to the point of joining the abolition movement. This was, of course, Douglass's intent as well as the intent of Garrison and other leaders of the movement. However, Douglass had more to say than that. He did not want to make the case that slavery was evil and should be abolished *only* because slaves were treated so abysmally. He aimed to make a much deeper, subtler, and ultimately more political case.

After reading the *Narrative*, readers might come away with the idea that slavery could be justified if slaves were treated more humanely. In fact, many Southern slaveholders and their abettors, as Douglass called them, already tried to justify slavery by claiming that most slave owners were kind and generous, and that most slaves were happy. This was rubbish, but a surprising number of people believed it.

In 1855, Douglass wrote a second biography. It was called *My Bondage and My Freedom*, and it clearly addressed this problem. In this book, Douglass took a different approach to his story. He described Sophia Auld, the woman who taught him the alphabet when he was a little boy, as a kind and tenderhearted woman. But he explained that her kindness and friendliness should not be misunderstood. He wrote:

> Nature had made us friends; slavery made us enemies … My feelings were not the result of any marked cruelty in the treatment I received; they sprung from the consideration of my being a slave at all. It was slavery—not its mere incidents—that I hated … The feeding and clothing me well, could not atone for taking my liberty from me. The smiles of

> my mistress could not remove the deep sorrow that dwelt in my young bosom. Indeed, these, in time, came only to deepen my sorrow. She had changed; and the reader will see that I had changed, too. We were both victims to the same overshadowing evil—she, as mistress, I as slave.[3]

Rather than simply describing the incidents in his life, as the *Narrative* had, he couched his story in a philosophical framework and made a much more political statement. *Bondage* aimed not just to generate tears and heaving breasts in its readers, but to make readers think, carefully and logically, about what slavery did to the people who were enslaved, what it did to the people who enslaved them, and what it did to the society that allowed slavery to exist. In it, Douglass made it quite clear that both slave and slave owner were damaged by slavery—and by extension so were any people, or any nation, that allowed slavery.

This statement is made perhaps most strongly by a letter first published in the *North Star* but reprinted at the end of *Bondage*. It was a letter from Douglass to his former master, Thomas Auld, written after Douglass's freedom had been purchased. The letter is long and moving. Douglass asks Auld for news of Douglass's sisters, who were, as far as he knew, still being held in slavery. He then explains why he ran away—giving a great deal of the same kind of painful details that made the *Narrative* so powerful. He then asks Auld to imagine his own daughter being treated as Douglass's sisters were. Perhaps the most heartbreaking part of the letter is when Douglass tells Auld of his own children who had been born after he escaped, born in freedom. Douglass writes, "They are all in comfortable beds, and are sound asleep, perfectly secure under my own roof. There are no slaveholders here to rend my heart by snatching them from my arms or blast a mother's dearest hopes by tearing them from her bosom." But it is the end of the letter that truly shows Douglass's humanity and contrasts it so powerfully with the man who enslaved him and continued to enslave his relatives and friends. He expresses a genuine sympathy for his former master, indicating that the weight of such an evil must be a hard thing to bear, and explains to him what it is for a human to truly serve another:

> Your mind must have become darkened, your heart hardened, your conscience seared and petrified, or you would have long since thrown off the accursed load and sought relief at the hands of a sin-forgiving God ... I entertain no malice towards you personally. There is no roof under which you would be more safe than mine, and there is nothing in my house which you might need for your comfort, which I would not readily grant. Indeed, I should esteem it a privilege, to set you an example as to how mankind ought to treat each other. I am your fellow man, but not your slave.[4]

Give Us the Facts

Douglass was clearly now much more than a former slave with remarkable oratorical and writing skills. He was a public intellectual. If his eloquence had initially made some people doubt he was really a former slave, it was that same eloquence that convinced a great portion of the public of the true evils of slavery. Before Douglass, many people—even in the North—were not convinced that slaves were capable of being citizens.

Because slaves were not allowed to get an education—even to learn to read and write—it was easy for people to underestimate their intelligence. Most people in the North had very little contact with slaves or even with free African Americans. Many of the people who approved of abolition were still not prepared to go as far as Garrison and Douglass in calling for full citizenship rights for former slaves. Douglass's experience when he arrived in New Bedford and tried to find work as a caulker, a trade in which he had experience and qualifications, was a glaring example that an end to slavery did not necessarily mean an end to prejudice. Southerners treated slaves as if they were farm animals and seemed to think they had little more intelligence and feeling than animals—perhaps even less so. Northerners may not have gone that far, but for the most part, they did believe that black people were intellectually inferior to whites. They may have wanted to end the practice of slavery, but extending the right to full political participation in the nation was a bit too much.

Douglass—by his very existence—was a powerful counterargument to this position. Clearly this was a man who was as well if not better educated than many of his fellow Americans, white or black. Against long odds and at great personal risk, he had taught himself to read (after a little head start from Mrs. Auld) and used that skill to further educate himself.

Though they no doubt meant well, Garrison and those in his organization often used Douglass as a living example of the horrors of slavery. Douglass told of his life as a slave, and at the same time amazed audiences with his oratorical ability. Garrison once described the effect Douglass had on audiences by saying that they reacted as if they were seeing a donkey suddenly begin to talk.

FOLLOW THE NORTH STAR

Like its inspiration the *Liberator*, the *North Star* was dedicated to ending slavery by educating readers about the institution and informing them how it might be abolished. It was one of the first African American–owned businesses in the United States. The *North Star* advocated a nonviolent approach, but unlike Garrison's paper, Douglass's publication encouraged political engagement.

Though there were several papers at the time that argued for abolition, Douglass's was the first to be owned and operated by a former slave. It was a popular paper, but it was not financially successful. Douglass supported the venture with speaking fees from his lecture, and at one time he even borrowed money on his house to help the paper meet its expenses. In 1851, owing to financial difficulties, the *North Star* merged with the paper of the Liberty Party (a political party that supported abolition) and took the name *Frederick Douglass's Paper*. Many people contributed to Douglass's papers over the years, including on at least one occasion the British novelist Charles Dickens.

In his second book, Douglass recalls John Collins, one of the leaders of the Massachusetts Anti-Slavery Society, advising him to "give us the facts ... we will take care of the philosophy."[5] But Douglass had quite a lot of philosophy to offer, and as the nation inched toward war, his intellect and his philosophy would be sorely needed.

The drumbeat of war was increasing as the nation tore itself apart over slavery. It was in this environment that Douglass released his second autobiography. He continued to lecture and write regularly for his own newspaper, the *North Star*, as well as for other publications. In his writing and his lectures he made a strong case for abolition, but he did much more than that.

Douglass's last autobiography, *The Life and Times of Frederick Douglass*, was not published until 1881, fourteen years before his death and long after the end of the Civil War. By this time, slaves were free and black men had the right to vote. However, this book gave interesting insight into Douglass's thinking during the years before emancipation. He discussed his relationship with John Brown and the complexities of Brown's belief in the need for a violent response to slavery. Douglass also demonstrated an amazing understanding of the nation's struggle over the issue of slavery and how slavery was the central fault line that would split the nation in two.

The original edition of *Life and Times* began with an introduction by George Lewis Ruffin. Ruffin was the first African American graduate of Harvard Law School and the first African American judge in the United States. He described Douglass as "one of the foremost orators of the age ... a writer of power and elegance of expression; a thinker whose views are potent in controlling and shaping public opinion ... a cultivated gentleman whose virtues as a husband, father, and citizen are the highest honor a man can have."[6]

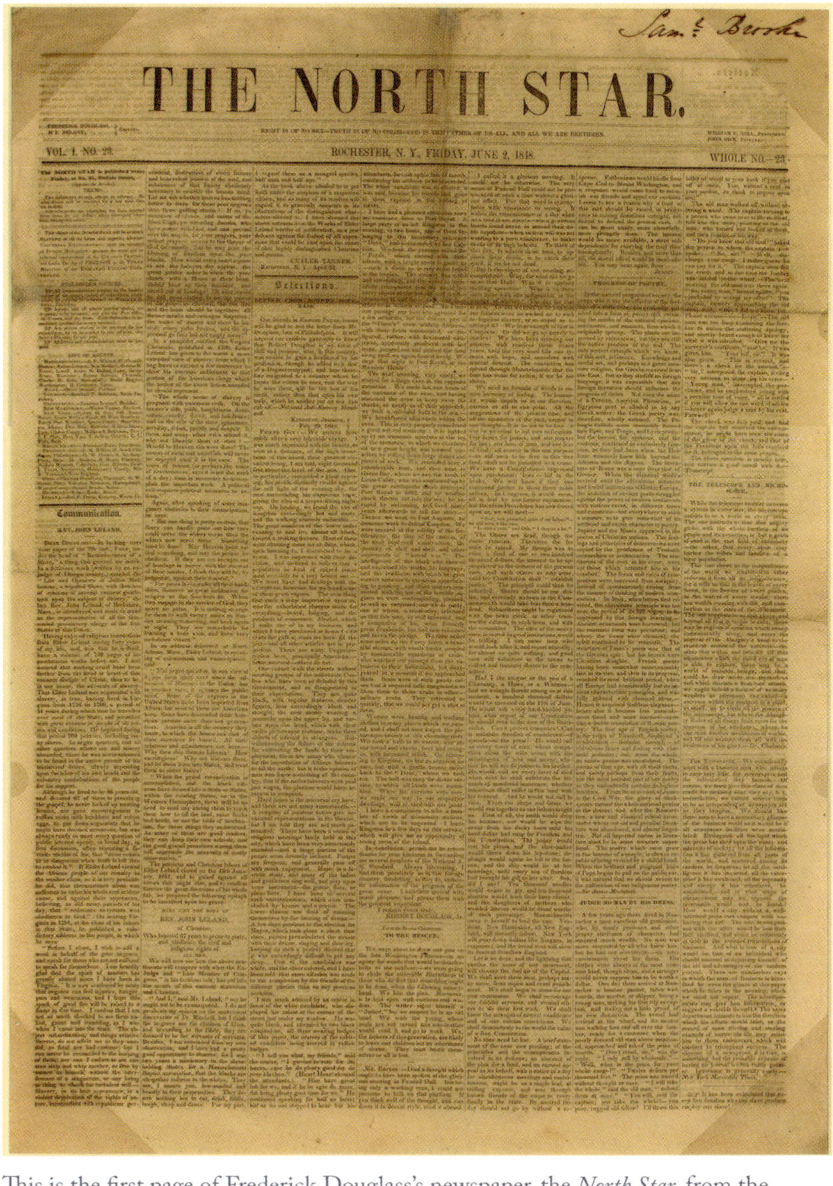

THE NORTH STAR.

VOL. I. NO. 23. ROCHESTER, N. Y., FRIDAY, JUNE 2, 1848. WHOLE NO.—23.

This is the first page of Frederick Douglass's newspaper, the *North Star*, from the June 2, 1848, edition.

Douglass had indeed come a long way from being urged onto the podium with the reminder to leave the philosophy to others.

Prelude to War

By the time Douglass wrote *Bondage* in 1855, slavery had become a serious and divisive political issue. The Compromise of 1850 included a new Fugitive Slave Act. This one was much stronger than the original Fugitive Slave Act, passed in 1793. The 1850 law imposed very high fines on officials who did not arrest runaway slaves, and people who aided runaway slaves in any way could be put in jail. This made it very dangerous not only for escaped slaves but for free people who helped them in any way, such as people who worked with the Underground Railroad. In exchange for this draconian law, it was agreed that slavery would not be expanded to the new state of California. However, two new territories, New Mexico and Utah, were created at the same time. The agreement was that those territories, should they become states, would decide through popular sovereignty whether they would be slave or free. Popular sovereignty meant that whichever opinion the majority of people living in a territory held on a matter would become the law after a vote. The Fugitive Slave Act had led to a great many well-publicized captures of runaway slaves (and a few dramatic rescues), and had the perhaps unsurprising effect of generating more sympathy for the abolitionist cause—though it also did a great deal of damage.

In 1852, abolitionist Harriet Beecher Stowe inflamed passions still further with the publication of *Uncle Tom's Cabin*. The book was a fictional account of the lives of slaves. It sold well and had an effect similar to that of Douglass's *Narrative*, in that it aroused the conscience of a large part of the nation.

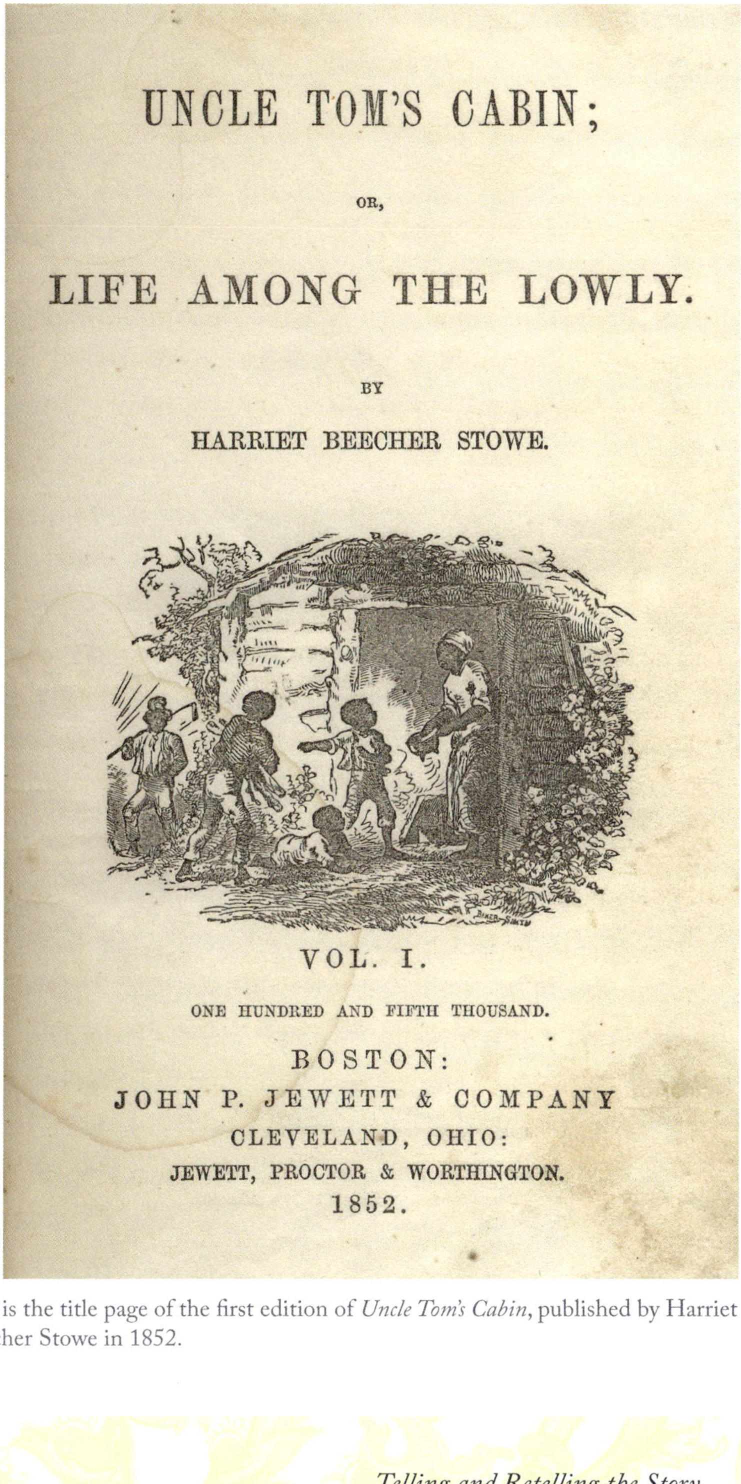

UNCLE TOM'S CABIN;

OR,

LIFE AMONG THE LOWLY.

BY

HARRIET BEECHER STOWE.

VOL. I.

ONE HUNDRED AND FIFTH THOUSAND.

BOSTON:

JOHN P. JEWETT & COMPANY

CLEVELAND, OHIO:

JEWETT, PROCTOR & WORTHINGTON.

1852.

This is the title page of the first edition of *Uncle Tom's Cabin*, published by Harriet Beecher Stowe in 1852.

However, slaveholders and their supporters were outraged, claiming the book was sentimental propaganda that defamed the South and slaveholders.

Then in 1854, the Kansas-Nebraska Act overturned the Missouri Compromise of 1820 by stating that new territories could decide by popular vote if they wanted to be slave states or free. (The Fugitive Slave Act remained in force, however.) In Kansas, outbreaks of violence between pro- and antislavery factions provided a prelude to the Civil War. These bloody skirmishes became so common that the territory earned the nickname "Bleeding Kansas."

Meanwhile, Douglass continued to insist that no compromises and no decisions about the self-determination in the territories would solve this problem. The nation could not last as long as slavery was a part of it. It is not clear how much of this message came through at the time, and it is certain that it was watered down in later years when the nation, both South and North, preferred to look back on the Civil War as a tragic misunderstanding brought about by an unwillingness to compromise, rather than a war that had to be fought to free four million people and save the soul of a nation. But modern readers are beginning to see what Douglass was trying to get across. In a 2014 article for the *Atlantic* (a magazine Douglass himself wrote for on many occasions), writer Ta-Nehisi Coates said this about Douglass's autobiographies: "Douglass is a masterful narrator, and one of the things he communicates is that slavery is not a sanitized form of forced labor, but first and foremost, a system of violence, an assault on black bodies, black families, and black institutions." Even in those cases when slaves are not subject to overt acts of physical violence, they are victims of violence, Douglass argued. Or as Coates put it, "You can not plunder a people nonviolently."[7]

However, the plundering of a people would not be put right without a war—and for a time it seemed as if even the war would not achieve that end. Douglass still had a lot of work to do, and the next phase of it would require him not only to speak out about slavery from the podium and his newspaper, but to also do so across the desk and over a cup of tea with a man who would become a good friend.

CHAPTER FIVE

Speaking Truth to Power

As the nation moved into war, the need to make a strong case for abolition became even more urgent. The Civil War provided a new opportunity for ending slavery once and for all. However, it was by no means given that the United States would win the war—or even if it did that restoring the Union would mean the end of slavery, much less equal rights for African Americans. It was at this point in his career that Douglass faced his greatest challenge since he had escaped from slavery. He had to help his nation win a war and convince both the nation and its leaders that the nation could not survive as long as slavery existed.

This photo of Abraham Lincoln was taken in the 1860s.

A Split in the Party

Slavery was the primary issue in the 1860 presidential election. Americans had been arguing about it for many years. Now the nation was on the verge of destruction because of it. Many people wondered how long the nation could survive half free and half slave. Some thought that slavery was a moral abomination and should simply be outlawed in all states and territories. Others didn't think half the nation had the right to tell the other half that it was morally wrong to own slaves. Whoever won the election of 1860 was going to face a greater challenge than any president before him ever had.

Leading up to the election, the Democrats were the majority party, but the issue of slavery split them as it would soon split the nation. Northern Democrats were not strongly opposed to slavery, but they didn't want slavery to expand to the Western territories. This was not so much because they abhorred the institution. Rather, the party drew its support primarily from working-class whites who didn't want to have to compete with slave labor. They ran candidate Stephen Douglas. Douglas was not a slave owner (though his wife was, and he had certainly benefited from the advantages of having slaves). Throughout his political career, he had worked hard for some kind of compromise that would preserve the Union and prevent war. He favored the idea of "popular sovereignty," the principle of letting the people who lived in a territory decide if slavery would be allowed there. However, as many a politician has discovered, trying to find a path that pleases everyone often results in pleasing no one. Stephen Douglas managed to alienate both Northern abolitionists, who thought he was too soft on slavery, and Southern Democrats, who thought his policies would eventually result in slavery's end.

Stephen Douglas worked hard for many years to help the United States reach a compromise on the issue of slavery.

Proslavery Southern Democrats split off from the party and ran John C. Breckinridge, a native of Kentucky, a slave state. Breckinridge was then vice president, serving with James Buchanan. Breckinridge believed that slaves were property, and thus ownership of them was protected by the Constitution. He said that Congress had no right to outlaw slavery or interfere in any way with the practice. Even so, he had been a moderate on the issue generally. When he was in Congress he had supported Stephen Douglas's popular sovereignty position. Now, however, he was running as the candidate of a party that supported the enforcement of the Fugitive Slave Act and the expansion of slavery into new states as they were admitted to the Union. His frequent comments about preserving the Union cost him some votes in the proslavery South.

John Bell of Tennessee, a former Speaker of the House, ran on the ticket of the Constitutional Union Party, which existed only for this election. He carried only three states, in the upper South, and did not have much of an impact on the election, except to further split the anti-Republican vote.

"I Have Always Hated Slavery"

The Republican Party, which had been founded in 1854 as a party that opposed expansion of slavery and supported its ultimate abolition, ran Abraham Lincoln. Lincoln's position on slavery at this time in his career can be a bit difficult to decipher. Though the Southern states were sure that his election meant certain abolition, he didn't run on an abolition platform. He was opposed to the expansion of slavery but did not advocate immediate emancipation. He was a gradualist, and was genuinely interested in finding a way to save the Union, whether that meant with slavery or without it—or at least that was what it sounded like from his public comments during this period.

In a speech in Chicago, Illinois, in 1858, he said, "I have always hated slavery, I think as much as any Abolitionist." But in very nearly the next breath, he clarified that view somewhat, "I have said a hundred times, and I have now no inclination to take it back, that I believe there is no right, and ought to be no inclination in the people of the free States to enter into the slave States, and interfere with the question of slavery at all."[1] So he seemed to believe that slavery was a bad thing, but the United States was stuck with it until and unless it died a natural death.

In any case, the subtleties didn't matter to the proslavery faction, who believed that limiting the expansion of slavery would as good as kill it. Once there were more antislavery representatives than proslavery representatives in Congress, slavery would be outlawed everywhere, they feared. Whether or not they were right about the effects of limiting the expansion of slavery, they were almost certainly right about Lincoln. But that wasn't obvious at first.

Had Lincoln needed the South to win, he would never have been president. No matter how moderate he may have seemed to abolitionists, to slave owners he and the Republican Party were the enemy. He won easily only because the opposition was so terribly divided. He won with no votes from any state that would be in the Confederacy, except Virginia, where he took a mere 1 percent of the vote. (He wasn't even on the ballot in the other soon-to-be Confederate states.)

Between Lincoln's election in November 1860 and his inauguration in March 1861, seven states had seceded from the United States and formed the Confederate States of America. One month later, Confederate forces fired on Fort Sumter, and the Civil War began.

The Radical and the Politician

Frederick Douglass supported Lincoln's candidacy wholeheartedly. During the winter months of 1860–1861 Douglass became quite frustrated at attempts by the United States government, and the Buchanan administration in particular, to prevent the South from seceding by assuring them that the inauguration of Lincoln would surely not mean the end of slavery. But this was all to no avail. As Douglass put it, "Happily for the cause of human freedom … the South was mad and would listen to no concessions."[2]

For many, and in fact for Lincoln, it would seem, the Civil War was primarily about restoring the Union and not about ending slavery. Douglass didn't see it this way. For him, the war was a tremendous opportunity to achieve freedom and equality for blacks. He made this position perfectly clear in a speech at the Cooper Institute in New York City in 1864:

> No war but an Abolition War; no peace but an Abolition Peace; liberty for all, chains for none; the black man a solider in war, a laborer in peace; a voter at the South as well as the North; America his permanent home, and all Americans his fellow countrymen. Such, fellow citizens, is my idea of the mission of the war.[3]

Douglass was an orator, a shaper of public opinion, and a radical. His job was to make the moral argument as clearly as it could be made and then hold the nation to those high standards.

Lincoln, on the other hand, was a politician. His job was much more pragmatic. If he wanted freedom and equality for blacks—and there is ample evidence that he very much did, even before he began to say it publicly—he had to do so very carefully. Even in the North, emancipation was still a divisive issue. By no means were all people in the free states in favor of ending slavery. Very few at all favored equality for blacks, even if they were granted their freedom. In fact, even though many opposed slavery, by far most Northerners were white supremacists. If Lincoln was going to restore the nation and achieve abolition, he had to persuade a reluctant nation, and he had to make the case with great delicacy. In addition, he realized that the Constitution protected slavery. Any move to abolish it had to work around that very big problem. Douglass could declaim and denounce. Lincoln had to govern.

For a time, Douglass wasn't much happier with Lincoln than the Southern states were. At a Fourth of July speech in 1862, Douglass pronounced Lincoln "no more fit for the place he holds than was James Buchanan," and said that Lincoln was a "miserable tool of traitors." Douglass's problem was that Lincoln had so far refused to declare emancipation for slaves that had escaped to the Union Army. Douglass thundered, "He has steadily refused to proclaim, as he has the constitutional and moral right to proclaim, complete emancipation to all slaves of rebels who should make their way into the lines of our army."[4]

Douglass did not, however, have long to wait. On January 1, 1863, Lincoln announced the Emancipation Proclamation. In many ways, the Emancipation Proclamation was more symbolic than anything else. It only freed slaves in the rebel states and not in the border states that had remained loyal. It also exempted the parts of the Confederacy that were under Northern control. Of course, that freedom would mean nothing if the United States did not win the war. It was, however, immensely powerful emotionally and changed the focus of the war. Where there had been doubt that this was a war for slavery, that doubt was now erased. More practically, the Emancipation Proclamation allowed black men to serve in the US Army and Navy. That would be a major factor in the United States eventually winning the war. Douglass's response was, "We shout for joy that we live to record this righteous decree!"[5] However, his happiness with Lincoln was not to last.

A Friendship Begins

Douglass worked hard for the United States war effort. He was too old to serve in the military, but he supported the cause by recruiting other free blacks to join. He ran an advertisement in his newspaper (now called *Douglass's Monthly*) soliciting black volunteers. The first to sign up was Douglass's own son, Charles Douglass. However, Douglass soon learned that blacks might be free to join the US military, but they certainly weren't equal there. Douglass's complaints were that black soldiers weren't paid as much as white soldiers and, more importantly, they took risks white soldiers didn't take. If a black soldier was captured by the Confederate Army, he was either executed or sold into slavery.

In August 1863, Douglass wrote a letter to George Stearns, the Massachusetts official responsible for recruiting black troops, and published it in his paper. Douglass told Stearns that he would no longer be recruiting black soldiers. He had discovered that "colored men have much overrated the enlightenment, justice, and generosity of our rulers in Washington."[6] The Union Army was becoming more and more dependent on black soldiers and could ill afford to lose Douglass's recruiting support. Stearns urged Douglass to go to Washington, DC, and take up the matter with the president himself. Douglass did just that.

This mural, painted in 1943 by William Edouard Scott, shows Douglass's first meeting with President Lincoln.

Douglass was both surprised and gratified by the way he was received by Lincoln—a man he had not always been kind to in his speeches and editorials. But the president greeted him warmly and respectfully. "Happily for me, there was no vain pomp and ceremony about him," Douglass recalled in his later autobiography. "I was never more quickly or more completely put at ease in the presence of a great man than in that of Abraham Lincoln."[7] Lincoln responded to Douglass's concerns in as noncommittal a way as you might expect from such as skilled politician, but he did hear him out.

The president vaguely assured Douglass that if the secretary of war recommended any black soldier for a promotion, he would certainly sign the commission. Lincoln had actually already signed Order 252, a move that was intended to offer some protection to black men taken as prisoners of war by the rebels. It said that for every black prisoner killed by the Confederates, the United States would execute one captured rebel solider. For every black soldier sold into slavery, the United States would force one rebel captive to do hard labor at public works. This was difficult to put into practice for a variety of reasons, not the least that the Confederacy did not acknowledge black soldiers as legitimate prisoners of war, so it was nigh impossible for US officials to know when they were taken. Order 252 was, however, a powerful statement of the nation's support for and gratitude to its black troops. Other of Douglass's concerns Lincoln did not address so directly, if at all. Lincoln left it to Congress to make the decision about equal pay. It was not until June 1864 that legislation passed, giving equal pay to black members of the military. It allowed for back pay for the years they had been underpaid.

However, on a personal level, the meeting was a huge success, and undoubtedly contributed in some way to Lincoln's approach to the rest of the war. It was the beginning of a true friendship between the two men as well. Douglass and Lincoln had much more in common than one might think. Both men were self-educated. Both had children and were devoted family men, and both had lost a beloved child (Douglass's daughter Annie had died in 1860, at ten years old; Lincoln's son Willie had died in 1862, age eleven). Both were lovers of language, and great writers and speakers. It turned out that they had learned to read from mostly the same books: the Bible, the works of William Shakespeare, and yes, *The Columbian Orator*. Douglass said of the meeting, "Though I was not entirely satisfied with his views, I was so well satisfied with the man … that I determined to go on with the recruiting."[8]

Hope Almost Lost

Douglass did carry on with his recruiting efforts. Then, in 1864, he had another meeting with the president. At the first meeting, Douglass had not been sure if he would be welcomed by Lincoln. This time he had no such worries. The president had sent a telegram to Douglass asking him to come to Washington, DC. Historian John Stauffer describes the meeting in his book *Giants: The Parallel Lives of Frederick Douglass and Abraham Lincoln*, which influenced the following recounting.

When Douglass reached the White House, Lincoln explained he was running for reelection and was afraid that he might lose to the Democratic candidate, George McClellan. McClellan was running on a peace platform. He favored a negotiated settlement with the Confederacy, in which the Confederate states would be allowed to remain a separate nation. Of course, any settlement the Confederate States of America was willing to accept would certainly allow them to

THE WOODHULL-DOUGLASS TICKET

Frederick Douglass was both a gadfly and advisor to presidents, especially Abraham Lincoln, one of the greatest presidents the United States has ever had. Douglass himself never sought office. He was, however, a vice presidential candidate once.

In 1872—seven years after the Civil War ended and forty-eight years before the Nineteenth Amendment gave women the right to vote—Victoria Woodhull ran for president of the United States. Woodhull was a women's rights advocate who owned a newspaper and a stock brokerage. At one time, she had also been a fortune teller. She was the candidate of the Equal Rights Party, a party she had helped form. The party nominated Frederick Douglass as her running mate. Douglass did not accept the nomination. As far as we know, he did not even acknowledge it.

Woodhull was an outspoken advocate for free love—it meant that women should have a choice about who they marry and the right to divorce a husband if they choose. She was arrested for violating morality laws and was in jail on Election Day. It didn't matter much where she was that day, nor that her running mate was not on board with the campaign, for it's uncertain whether her name appeared on the ballot in any state. Because of this, we don't know how many votes she received, if any. However, Woodhull's ambitions were truly remarkable for the time.

Victoria Woodhull posed for this photograph in 1872. Later, she would be an inspiration to many women who wanted to break barriers in politics.

This photograph shows President Lincoln (*right of center, at the podium*) giving his second inaugural address in 1865. Frederick Douglass was an invited guest.

keep slavery intact. The Union was weary of war and not that committed to ending slavery in the South. The population was ready to be done with the rebels once and for all. McClellan had a good chance of defeating Lincoln. If he did win, the hopes of both Douglass and Lincoln would be dashed. Lincoln would lose his hope of saving the nation. Douglass would lose the hope of abolishing slavery. If the Confederate States of America was allowed to be a separate nation, there was very little the United States could do to end slavery there.

Lincoln's plan was for Douglass to take a few handpicked black soldiers on a raid into the South and bring back as many black soldiers as they could. They would form these men into a regiment that would then, being highly motivated, go back into the South and win a major military victory, thus convincing voters that the war was winnable, and soon. This was oddly like John Brown's plan, but far more well designed, and it certainly would be much better funded. Once again, Douglass discussed and advised, but he did not end up taking part in this plan. In fact, the plan was not needed after all.

The idea that Lincoln even considered such a drastic plan to win the war and free the slaves impressed Douglass greatly. And Douglass did all he could to help reelect the man he had once said was not fit for the office. "Regarding, as I did, the continuance of the war and the complete suppression of the rebellion and the retention in office of President Lincoln as essential to the total destruction of slavery, I certainly exerted myself to the uttermost in my small way to secure his reelection," he wrote.[9] Lincoln had worried in vain. The efforts of Union generals Ulysses S. Grant and William T. Sherman began to turn the war around well before November, and Lincoln won reelection easily.

The next time the two men would meet would be at Lincoln's second inauguration, in March 1865. It was the first time an African American had attended a presidential inauguration reception. Douglass was detained at the door because he was black. When he finally did get in to see Lincoln, the president greeted him warmly, reaching out for Douglass's hand and saying to the crowd, "Here comes my friend Frederick Douglass." Lincoln asked what Douglass had thought of his speech, saying, "There is no man in the country whose opinion I value more than yours."[10]

Throughout the war, Douglass had worked tirelessly to convince the nation that the Civil War was a war to end slavery and not merely to preserve the Union. It was a war for the soul of the nation. Now the nation was saved. In December 1865, the Thirteenth Amendment to the Constitution was ratified, making slavery illegal once and for all. Douglass's work on abolition was done. However, his work for social justice would continue.

CHAPTER SIX

That Great Leonine Gaze

Frederick Douglass wanted freedom and equality not just for former slaves and African Americans, but for all people everywhere. Once slaves had been freed, he spent the rest of his life working to help them gain social, political, and economic equality, and working to that end for everyone else as well. His work continues even today, as he still inspires the many people who are working for social justice for all of humanity.

The Work Continues

After the war was over, Douglass received many invitations to speak at colleges and meetings of many different organizations. At first these invitations intimidated him.

This portrait of Douglass was taken sometime around 1850, when he was working toward the abolition of slavery.

He wasn't sure what to say. His old antislavery speeches were no longer needed. However, he soon found his post-emancipation voice. Douglass realized that life for freed slaves and all African Americans would not be easy—particularly in the South, where they were already facing resistance and discrimination. His emphasis shifted from demanding freedom for his people to demanding equality for them. He also offered newly freed slaves guidance in living in this new, post-slavery world.

In his oft-requested lecture "Self Made Men," Douglass spoke of "men who are not brought up but who are obliged to come up, not only without the voluntary assistance or friendly co-operation of society, but often in open and derisive defiance of all the efforts of society and the tendency of circumstances to repress and keep them down." The man who had taught himself to read and carefully planned and executed his escape from slavery advised the newly freed not to depend on chance to improve their lives and not to count on other people to be of much help either. He encouraged them to be self-made men, as he was. The wise man, he said, "knows that health is maintained by right living; that disease is cured by the right use of remedies; that bread is produced by tilling the soil; that knowledge is obtained by study; that wealth is secured by saving and that battles are won by fighting. To him, the lazy man is the unlucky man and the man of luck the man of work." Douglass never suggested that freedom from slavery meant the fight was over.[1]

Douglass also realized that the condition of blacks would not continue to improve until they were granted not just emancipation but full citizenship. The Thirteenth Amendment freed blacks from slavery, but that was not enough. In 1866, Douglass wrote to President Andrew Johnson, who had become president after Lincoln was assassinated in April 1865, arguing for voting rights for blacks. "If the Negro knows enough to fight for his country," he wrote, "he knows enough to vote; if he knows enough to pay taxes for the support of the government, he knows enough to vote."[2] In 1870, the nation agreed with him, and ratified the Fifteenth Amendment, giving black men the right to vote. But the world was still not a welcoming or easy place for African Americans. Southern states made every effort to deny newly freed blacks their rights, and the rest of the nation did not open its arms too widely to their new fellow citizens.

Liberty and Justice for All

In 1852, nine years before the beginning of the Civil War, Frederick Douglass had spoken to the Ladies' Anti-Slavery Society at Corinthian Hall in Rochester, New York. It was July 5, the day after the nation had celebrated the signing of the US Declaration of Independence, a document that states "all men are created equal." Douglass had been asked to deliver a Fourth of July oration. His speech, later published under the title "What to the Slave is the Fourth of July?," does not celebrate the independence of the colonies from England. Instead he points out that he and his fellow African Americans, slave and free, are not included in this wonderful anniversary: "Fellow-citizens; above your national, tumultuous joy, I hear the mournful wail of millions!" He said that to the slave, the celebration is "a sham."[3]

Later, after slavery was abolished, Americans black and white still had to work to make sure those words "all men are created equal" were not a sham. Douglass became a voice and a leader for the black communities in the South and the North as they continued to struggle and work for their freedom, holding the nation to its promise of freedom and equality, of liberty and justice for all.

This photograph shows workers rebuilding the ruins of the South after the Civil War.

Douglass did not just work on behalf of justice for former slaves and other African Americans. He also became a powerful voice in the fight for women's rights. He was one of very few men who attended the 1848 Seneca Falls Convention that launched the women's rights movement. He was one of the signers of the Declaration of Sentiments, the document drafted at Seneca Falls that stated the demands of the women's movement. Douglass took great pride in his position on women's rights and was as staunch an advocate for women of all colors as he was for blacks. He wrote, "I have never yet been able to find one consideration, one argument, or suggestion in favor of man's right to participate in civil government which did not equally apply to the right of woman."[4]

Most of the leaders of the women's movement—women like Susan B. Anthony, Elizabeth Cady Stanton, and Lucretia Mott—were also very active in the abolition movement. However, the two movements split over the Fifteenth Amendment, which gave black men the right to vote. Some women's rights supporters, including Stanton and Sojourner Truth, refused to support the amendment if it did not give the vote to women as well as to black men. Douglass believed that women already had at least some say in politics because their husbands could vote. It is also likely that he, as another great leader would advise many years later, did not want to let the perfect be the enemy of the good. Despite this disagreement, Douglass was still an active supporter of women's rights for the rest of his life.

Though the fight for equality for blacks was just beginning, Douglass's service to his country did not go unrewarded. He was greatly respected by all who knew him. He worked on several presidential campaigns, including those of Ulysses S. Grant, former Civil War general. He served as US Marshal

Susan B. Anthony, a women's rights activist and an abolitionist, worked closely with Douglass on these issues.

This house was Frederick Douglass's home in Washington, DC. He died there a free man, serving no one but his country. Today, the house is an important historic landmark.

of the District of Columbia. This position had to be approved by the US Senate. Douglass's approval was the first time the Senate had approved a black man for any position. Later, he served two years as the US consul general to Haiti. Douglass had moved from Rochester, New York, to Washington, DC, in 1872. His house near the capital was a beautiful columned home, called Cedar Hill House. There is some pleasant irony in the fact that Frederick Douglass, born a slave, spent his final years in a lovely home that looked not unlike the houses of slaveholders in the antebellum South. However, there were no slaves here, only a man who served no one but his country, and as a free citizen.

A Mighty Gaze

The story of Frederick Douglass is remarkable in so many ways. This man was born a slave, who owned nothing, not even himself. He was given no education; he was forbidden even to learn to read. Yet he found a way to learn anyway.

BEING RECOGNIZED MORE AND MORE

In 1936, the city of Nashville, Tennessee, planned to open a new park and name it in honor of Frederick Douglass. Many white citizens in the city did not want to honor the abolitionist and civil rights activist by naming the park after him. So, the city shortened the name of the park to Fred Douglas Park, and left off the last *s*. Soon it came to be known as simply Douglas Park. The children who played there and the visitors who came to read a book or stroll in the park did not learn the story of the great man the park was intended to honor.

Then, in February 2017, newly elected president Donald Trump mentioned Douglass in the president's statement for Black History Month. Trump said that Douglass was being recognized more and more. This caused David Ewing, a lawyer and historian living in Nashville, to wonder if Douglas Park was named after Frederick Douglass. Ewing did a little research and discovered the whole story. He brought the matter to the attention of Nashville's mayor, Megan Barry. She acted quickly, and in March 2017, the mistake was corrected. The park was re-dedicated as Frederick Douglass Park later that month.

He overheard words of his master that showed him very clearly that the route to freedom was learning. He embraced learning and found his way to freedom. Once there, he kept learning and reading—and writing and talking. He gave thundering speeches to crowds and quiet advice in private. He raised a family, built a business, and took part in the government of his country. But we do him and ourselves an injustice if we dismiss Frederick Douglass as a unique example of a human being. He proved that immense obstacles can be overcome, and he showed us how we can overcome obstacles too.

In September 2016, at the opening of the National Museum of African American History and Culture in Washington, DC, President Barack Obama spoke of African American history and of Frederick Douglass:

> Yes, African Americans have felt the cold weight of shackles and the stinging lash of the field whip. But we've also dared to run north and sing songs from Harriet Tubman's hymnal. We've buttoned up our Union blues to join the fight for our freedom, we've railed against injustice for decade upon decade, a lifetime of struggle and progress and enlightenment that we see etched in Frederick Douglass's mighty leonine gaze.[5]

That mighty gaze is still upon us today. Douglass learned when the Civil War was over and the slaves were freed that his work was not done. His voice still booms down through the years to us today, reminding us that we must not stop working, struggling, fighting for justice. Douglass reminds us, "This struggle may be a moral one, or it may be a physical one, and it may be both moral and physical, but it must be a struggle.

Frederick Douglass (*right*) appears here, near the end of his life, with his grandson Joseph Douglass (*left*), a concert violinist.

Power concedes nothing without a demand. It never did and it never will."[6] If, as that struggle goes on, we need comfort and strength, motivation and inspiration, we need only to look back to Frederick Douglass.

Douglass knew the power of language. He knew that education was the key not only to his own freedom but to that of all his fellow slaves, and it was the key to improving the lives of free people as well. Learning to read, reading the works of many thinkers who had come before him, learning to make an argument and express it with grace and power, these were the tools Frederick Douglass used to claim his life as his own, and to change the course of a nation. And he left us these tools to use today.

CHRONOLOGY

1818 Frederick Douglass is born in Tuckahoe, Talbot County, Maryland.

1838 Douglass escapes from slavery and goes to New York, then New Bedford, Massachusetts. He marries Anna Murray, a free black woman.

1839 Douglass subscribes to the *Liberator*. His first child, daughter Rosetta, is born.

1840 Douglass's oldest son, Lewis Douglass, is born.

1841 Douglass speaks at a meeting of the Massachusetts Anti-Slavery Society and becomes a regular speaker for the organization.

1842 Douglass and Anna's second son, Frederick Douglass Jr., is born.

1844 Charles Douglass, the Douglasses' third son, is born.

1845 Douglass publishes his first autobiography, *Narrative of the Life of Frederick Douglass, an American Slave*. Goes to England to avoid capture and lectures there.

1846 Friends in Europe raise the funds and buy Douglass's freedom; he returns to the United States.

1847 Douglass moves with his family to Rochester, New York. He publishes the first issue of the *North Star* also that year.

1848 Douglass attends the first Women's Rights Convention in Seneca Falls, New York. His daughter Annie is born.

1851 The *North Star* merges with the *Liberty Party Paper* and becomes *Frederick Douglass's Paper.*

1855 Douglass publishes his second autobiography, *My Bondage and My Freedom*.

1859 Douglass's ten-year-old daughter, Annie, dies. He is in Glasgow, Scotland, at this time, laying low after John Brown's raid.

1860 Abraham Lincoln is elected president.

1861 The Civil War begins.

1863 Douglass visits Lincoln in Washington, DC. Lincoln signs the Emancipation Proclamation.

1865 The Civil War ends. The Thirteenth Amendment to the United States Constitution ends slavery throughout the nation.

1870 The Fifteenth Amendment gives black men the right to vote.

1881 Douglass publishes his third autobiography, *The Life and Times of Frederick Douglass*.

1882 Anna Douglass dies.

1884 Douglass marries Helen Pitts, his second wife.

1895 Douglass dies of a heart attack at his home in Washington, DC.

GLOSSARY

abettor Someone who encourages or aids another in committing a crime or an immoral act.

abolitionist Someone who is in favor of and working toward ending the practice of slavery.

anarchist Someone who refuses to recognize any kind of political authority.

antebellum Before a war, particularly the period before the US Civil War.

articulate The ability to speak fluently and gracefully.

autobiography A biography written by the person who is the subject of the book.

baritone A deep male voice, between the tenor and the bass range.

caulker A person who seals holes in structures, like ships.

delegate A person who acts on behalf of others at a meeting or a convention.

denunciation A harsh, public condemnation of a person, idea, or institution.

draconian Excessively cruel or severe.

emancipation Liberation, particularly the freeing of someone from slavery.

equivocate To use vague language or arguments to avoid commitment to a position or cause.

exposé A factual, often journalistic report of shocking or disturbing events or situations.

inauguration The ceremony that officially begins the term of office of an official, such as the president.

instrumental Serving as a means of achieving a goal or an objective.

insurrection A fight against authority.

land speculator A person who buys land hoping it will sell for a higher value later on.

leonine Lion-like.

manumission The process of releasing someone from slavery.

mentor An older or more experienced person who advises and counsels others in his or her area of expertise.

noncommittal Not expressing or in any way indicating agreement or a promise of action.

orator A person who gives excellent speeches.

peruse To read a particular piece of writing thoroughly or carefully.

plantation A large, usually agricultural estate.

platform In politics, the set of positions or policies of a given party or candidate.

preface The opening section of a book, usually written by a person close to the author, but not the author themselves.

protégé Someone who receives career advice, support, and guidance from a more experienced, often older person.

ratify To officially agree to; to sign off on.

rhetoric The art of speaking or writing in such a way as to convince or persuade.

schism A rift or separation caused by deep differences in fundamental beliefs.

secede To withdraw from membership in a political (or religious) alliance or federation.

skirmish A small battle that takes place in a larger war.

supersede To replace.

supremacist Someone who believes that one group of people is superior to other groups.

SOURCES

CHAPTER ONE

1. Frederick Douglass, *Narrative of the Life of Frederick Douglass, an American Slave* (New York: Penguin, 2014), 18.

2. Ibid., 20.

3. US Government Printing Office, *Annual Report of the American Historical Association*, volume 2 (Washington, DC, 1900), 1178.

4. "The First Editorial of The Liberator (1 January 1831)," Oxford American Studies Center, http://0-www.oxfordaasc.com.vulcan.bham.lib.al.us/article/ps/ps-aasc-0031?hi=1&highlight=1&from=quick&pos=2#match.

5. The Constitution of the United States, Article IV, section 2.

6. "Letter from Frederick Douglass to Harriet Tubman, 1868," Harriet Tubman Historical Society, http://www.harriet-tubman.org/letter-from-frederick-douglass.

CHAPTER TWO

1. Douglass, *Narrative*, 17.

2. Frederick Douglass, *The Illustrated Edition of the Life and Times of Frederick Douglass* (introduction by Henry Louis Gates, Jr.), (Minneapolis, MN: Zenith, 2015), 3.

3. Ibid., 38.

4. Frederick Douglass, *My Bondage and My Freedom*, ed. David W. Blight (New Haven, CT: Yale University Press, 2014), 217.

5. Douglass, *Narrative*, 105.

6. Ibid., 105–106.

7. *Liberator*, Accessible Archives, http://www.accessible-archives.com/collections/the-liberator.

8. Ibid.

9. Douglass, *Narrative*, 107.

10. Douglass, *Illustrated Life and Times*, 102.

CHAPTER THREE

1. University of Delaware Library, "The Liberator," https://library.udel.edu/databases/liberator.

2. Douglass, *Bondage*, 285.

3. Ibid., 289.

4. Douglass, *Illustrated Life and Times*, 114.

5. Donald Yacovone, "A Covenant with Death and an Agreement with Hell," Massachusetts Historical Society, July 2005, http://www.masshist.org/object-of-the-month/objects/a-covenant-with-death-and-an-agreement-with-hell-2005-07-01.

6. Frederick Douglass, "The Constitution of the United States: Is It Pro-Slavery or Anti-Slavery?" Speech, Glasgow, Scotland, March 26, 1860, http://teachingamericanhistory.org/library/document/the-constitution-of-the-united-states-is-it-pro-slavery-or-anti-slavery.

7. Ibid.

8. William Lloyd Garrison, *The Letters of William Lloyd Garrison, Volume IV: From Disunion to the Brink of War: 1850–1860* (Cambridge, MA: Belknap, 1976), 256.

CHAPTER FOUR

1. Douglass, *Narrative*, 13–14.

2. Ibid., 7.

3. Douglass, *Bondage*, 130–131.

4. Ibid., 350–353

5. Ibid., 289.

6. George Lewis Ruffin, Introduction to *Life and Times of Frederick Douglass*, Frederick Douglass Heritage Society, http://www.frederick-douglass-heritage.org/life-and-times-of-frederick-douglass.

7. Ta-Nehisi Coates, "Slavery Made America," *Atlantic*, June 24, 2014. https://www.theatlantic.com/business/archive/2014/06/slavery-made-america/373288.

CHAPTER FIVE

1. Abraham Lincoln, Speech at Chicago, Illinois, July 10, 1858. *Collected Works of Abraham Lincoln, Vol II*, 492, https://quod.lib.umich.edu/l/lincoln.

2. Douglass, *Illustrated Life and Times*, 136.

3. Frederick Douglass, "The Mission of the War," speech, New York City, 1864, Blackpast.org, http://www.blackpast.org/1864-frederick-douglass-mission-war

4. Frederick Douglass, *The Essential Douglass: Selected Writings and Speeches*, ed. Nicholas Buccola (New York: Hackett, 2016), 176.

5. James McPherson, *Battle Cry of Freedom: The Civil War Era* (New York: Oxford University Press, 1988), 558.

6. Frederick Douglass, *Life and Times of Frederick Douglass: An African American Heritage Book* (Redford, VA: Wilder, 2008), 200.

7. Douglass, *Illustrated Life and Times*, 146.

8. Ibid., 147.

9. Ibid., 153.

10. James Oakes, *The Radical and the Republican: Frederick Douglass, Abraham Lincoln, and the Triumph of Antislavery Politics* (New York: W. W. Norton, 2007), 242.

CHAPTER SIX

1. Frederick Douglass, "Self-Made Men" (Speech, written in 1872), http://www.frederick-douglass-heritage.org/self-made-men.

2. "The Reconstruction Years and Civil Rights," Frederick Douglass Heritage, http://www.frederick-douglass-heritage.org/reconstruction-civil-rights.

3. Douglass, *Narrative*, 129.

4. Douglass, *Illustrated Life and Times*, 181.

5. Barack Obama, Remarks on the Opening of the National Museum of African American History and Culture, Washington, DC, September 24, 2016, http://time.com/4506800/barack-obama-african-american-history-museum-transcript.

6. Frederick Douglass, "If There Is No Struggle, There Is No Progress," speech, August 3, 1857, http://www.blackpast.org/1857-frederick-douglass-if-there-no-struggle-there-no-progress.

FURTHER INFORMATION

Douglass, Frederick. *The Essential Douglass: Selected Writings and Speeches*. Edited by Nicholas Buccola. New York: Hackett, 2016.

———. *The Illustrated Edition of the Life and Times of Frederick Douglass*. Minneapolis, MN: Zenith, 2015.

———. *Narrative of the Life of Frederick Douglass an American Slave*. Edited by Ira Dworkin. New York: Penguin, 2014.

Enzo, George. *The Civil War*. Primary Sources in US History. New York: Cavendish Square, 2015.

Grayson, Robert. *The US Civil War: Why They Fought*. North Mankato, MN: Capstone, 2016.

Smith, Adam I. P. *Abraham Lincoln*. History Makers. New York: Cavendish Square, 2017.

WEBSITES

Frederick Douglass Heritage Site
http://www.frederick-douglass-heritage.org

A wealth of information on Douglass, including speeches, writings, and free, searchable e-book versions of his autobiographies can be found here.

Frederick Douglass National Historic Site
https://www.nps.gov/frdo/index.htm

Maintained by the National Park Service, this site has information about Frederick Douglass, videos, and useful information for planning a trip to the site.

Frederick Douglass Project
http://rbscp.lib.rochester.edu/2494

This website details a project of the University of Rochester, with digitized writings of Frederick Douglass, including images and links to other useful sites.

MUSEUMS

Frederick Douglass Museum and Cultural Center ("Twin Oaks")
3200 Wayman Ave
Annapolis, MD 21403

National Museum of African American History and Culture
1400 Constitution Ave.
Washington, DC 20560

National Museum of American History
14th Street and Constitution Ave, NW
Washington, DC 20560

BIBLIOGRAPHY

Beard, Rick. "When Douglass Met Lincoln." *New York Times*, August 9, 2013. https://opinionator.blogs.nytimes.com/2013/08/09/when-douglass-met-lincoln.

Blakemore, Erin. "Five Things to Know About the Declaration of Sentiments." *Smithsonian*, June 8, 2016. https://www.smithsonianmag.com/smart-news/five-things-know-about-declaration-sentiments-180959352.

Blight, Dave. "Frederick Douglass, Refugee." *Atlantic*, February 7, 2017. https://www.theatlantic.com/politics/archive/2017/02/frederick-douglass-refugee/515853.

Bordewich, Fergus M. "How Lincoln Bested Douglas in Their Famous Debates." *Smithsonian*, September 2008. https://www.smithsonianmag.com/history/how-lincoln-bested-douglas-in-their-famous-debates-7558180.

Coates, Ta-Nehisi. "Frederick Douglass: A Women's Rights Man." *Atlantic*, September 30, 2011. https://www.theatlantic.com/personal/archive/2011/09/frederick-douglass-a-womens-rights-man/245977.

———. "Slavery Made America." *Atlantic*, June 24, 2014. https://www.theatlantic.com/business/archive/2014/06/slavery-made-america/373288.

Douglass, Frederick. *The Essential Douglass: Selected Writings and Speeches*. Edited by Nicholas Buccola. New York: Hackett, 2016.

———. *The Illustrated Edition of the Life and Times of Frederick Douglass*. Minneapolis, MN: Zenith, 2015.

———. *Narrative of the Life of Frederick Douglass an American Slave*. Edited by Ira Dworkin. New York: Penguin, 2014.

———. "Reconstruction." *Atlantic*, December 1866. https://www.theatlantic.com/magazine/archive/1866/12/reconstruction/304561.

———. "Self-Made Men," speech, written in 1872. http://www.frederick-douglass-heritage.org/self-made-men.

———. "What to the Slave is the Fourth of July?" Reprinted with an introduction by Dave Zirin. *Nation*, July 4, 2012. https://www.thenation.com/article/what-slave-fourth-july-frederick-douglass.

Foner, Eric. *The Fiery Trial: Abraham Lincoln and American Slavery*. New York: W. W. Norton, 2010.

———. *Nothing but Freedom: Emancipation and Its Legacy*. Baton Rouge, LA: Louisiana State University Press, 1983.

Garrison, William Lloyd. *The Letters of William Lloyd Garrison, Volume IV: From Disunion to the Brink of War: 1850–1860*. Cambridge, MA: Belknap, 1976.

Gates, Henry Louis, Jr., ed. *Lincoln on Race and Slavery*. Princeton, NJ: Princeton University Press, 2009.

———. "Slavery by the Numbers." *Root*, February 10, 2014. https://www.theroot.com/slavery-by-the-numbers-1790874492.

Gienapp, William E., ed. *This Fiery Trial: The Speeches and Writings of Abraham Lincoln*. Oxford, UK: Oxford University Press, 2002.

Hindley, Meredith. "The Man Who Came in Second: How John Breckinridge and the Democratic Party Lost the 1860 Election." *Humanities*, November/December 2011. https://www.neh.gov/humanities/2011/novemberdecember/feature/the-man-who-came-in-second.

Holzer, Harold. "Election Day 1860." *Smithsonian*, November 2008. https://www.smithsonianmag.com/history/election-day-1860-84266675.

Lewis, Danny. "Victoria Woodhull Ran for President Before Women Had the Right to Vote." *Smithsonian*, May 10, 2016. https://www.smithsonianmag.com/smart-news/victoria-woodhull-ran-for-president-before-women-had-the-right-to-vote-180959038.

McClintock, Russell. *Lincoln and the Decision for War: The Northern Response to Secession*. Chapel Hill, NC: University of North Carolina Press, 2008.

McDaniel, Caleb. "The Lives of Frederick Douglass," January 9, 2013. http://wcm1.web.rice.edu/lives-of-frederick-douglass.html.

McPherson, James. *Battle Cry of Freedom: The Civil War Era*. New York: Oxford University Press, 1988.

Oakes, James. *Freedom National: The Destruction of Slavery in the United States 1861–1865*. New York: W. W. Norton, 2013.

———. *The Radical and the Republican: Frederick Douglass, Abraham Lincoln, and the Triumph of Antislavery Politics*. New York: W. W. Norton, 2007.

———. *Scorpion's Sting: Antislavery and the Coming of the Civil War*. New York: W. W. Norton, 2014.

Obama, Barack. *The Audacity of Hope: Thoughts on Reclaiming the American Dream*. New York: Three Rivers Press, 2006.

Ransom. Roger. "Economics of the Civil War." *EH.Net Encyclopedia*. August 24, 2001. http://eh.net/encyclopedia/the-economics-of-the-civil-war.

Shank, Michael. "'Lincoln': Where Was Frederick Douglass?" *Washington Post*, November 28, 2012. https://www.washingtonpost.com/blogs/therootdc/post/lincoln-where-was-frederick-douglass/2012/11/28/212a4e76-3978-11e2-a263-f0ebffed2f15_blog.html?utm_term=.6219a62cecff.

Stauffer, John. *Giants: The Parallel Lives of Frederick Douglass and Abraham Lincoln*. New York: Hachette, 2008.

Stewart, Alexander. "How Is Frederick Douglass Relevant Today?" *Socialist*, March 7, 2014. http://www.thesocialist.us/how-is-frederick-douglass-relevant-today.

United States Government Bureau of the Census. *Population of the United States in 1860; Compiled from the Original Returns of the Eighth Census*. Washington, DC: Government Printing Office, 1864.

INDEX

Page numbers in **boldface** refer to images.

ABOUT THE AUTHOR

Avery Elizabeth Hurt is the author of many books for children and young adults, and particularly enjoys writing about history. She has always believed that the more we examine the past, the better we'll be able to shape the future, and has found Frederick Douglass to be an enormous inspiration in the campaign for social justice.